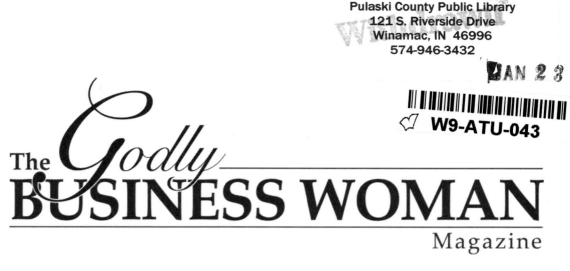

The *Godly*
BUSINESS WOMAN
Magazine

GUIDE TO COOKING
AND
ENTERTAINMENT

The *Godly* BUSINESS WOMAN
Magazine

GUIDE TO COOKING
AND
ENTERTAINMENT

Kathleen Jackson and Tracey Davison

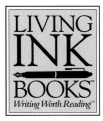

LIVING INK BOOKS
Writing Worth Reading

Published by AMG Publishers
6815 Shallowford Rd.
Chattanooga, TN 37421

ISBN 0-89957-153-0

First printing—July 2004

Cover designed by Jennifer Ross, Chattanooga, Tennessee
Interior design and typesetting by Reider Publishing Services, West Hollywood, California
Edited and Proofread by Melaine Rigney, Sharon Neal, Dan Penwell, and Warren Baker
Printed in the United States of America
09 08 07 06 05 04 –W– 8 7 6 5 4 3 2 1

To my husband, Royce Jackson, I dedicate this book to you for your wisdom, strength, honor, and unconditional love in every aspect of my life. Thank you for your prayers, support, and continual faith in me. Your solid walk with God is truly the foundation for our household, and I praise God for you.

To my daughter Michelle, you're a true example of Proverbs 22:6, "Train a child in the way he should go, and when he is old he will not turn from it." I am so proud of the wife and mother you have become. May God continue to bless your family as you open the doors of your home for the Lord's sake. Thank you for making me "nana."

—Kathleen Jackson, Publisher, *The Godly Business Woman Magazine*

To my husband, Andy Davison, for always being there for me and for making my world a brighter place. You have been my rock through this and every other endeavor in my life. Thank you for the godly example you are to our children and me.

To my children who are a blessing and inspiration to me—thank you for the wonderful joy you have already bestowed on my life and for the unending happiness I know is sure to come. You truly are gifts from God.

—Tracey Davison, Managing Editor, *The Godly Business Woman Magazine*

Contents

Section One
ENTERTAINING

Section Two
SPECIAL OCCASIONS

Section Three

HOLIDAYS AND FESTIVALS

Acknowledgments

"Honor one another above yourselves." (Rom. 12:10)

WHEN THIS PROJECT was started, we were the last two people on earth who thought we were right for this job. But God doesn't always go down the obvious road. "For I am the LORD, your God, who takes hold of your right hand and says to you, Do not fear; I will help you" (Isa. 41:13). To honor anyone in this book above the Lord would not seem appropriate, and our prayer is that the Lord will use the efforts of everyone involved to further His kingdom.

Yet, we want to honor those who assisted us throughout the process of creating this book. From conception to completion, it took nearly two years to actually bring this project to life, and we would like to thank those who gave of their time and talent to help us along the way. "Two are better than one, because they have a good return for their work: If one falls down, his friend can help him up. But pity the man who falls and has no one to help him up!" (Eccl. 4:9, 10). Without the cooperation of the following people, we could not have followed the path that God had created for us:

Vonette Bright, the "Queen of Hospitality," taught us how to use our home to serve others and how Jesus can be a part of any entertainment endeavor—down to the very last detail. From planning a simple or elaborate occasion to meal preparation and conversations over dinner, you have inspired us to use our homes for a deeper purpose. You're truly a blessing and wonderful role model and so deserving of the title "Queen of Hospitality." Thank you, Vonette, for your love and friendship, and for the warmth you added to this book.

Marita Littauer is a champion and friend to *The Godly Business Woman Magazine.* You have been an invaluable asset to us, and words cannot express our thanks for your generosity in sharing your knowledge of the industry with us throughout the development of this book.

Dan Penwell, the Product Development/Acquisitions Manager with AMG. From the moment this project was presented to you, we knew it was from God because of your love of cookbooks. Thank you for your continuous support, excitement, and enthusiasm about the potential of this book. Dan, you are a fine example of a godly businessman.

Warren Baker, Senior Editor with AMG. Without your expert knowledge of computers and computer graphics, the beautiful pictures in this book would have never happened. You have been an invaluable resource.

Eva Marie Everson, our friend, encourager, and another cheerleader for *The Godly Business Woman Magazine.* You have always been available to share your knowledge and ideas with us. You generously gave us valuable feedback and wise counsel on numerous occasions and without hesitation. Your southern belle upbringing was a blessing to us.

Melaine Rigney, our copy editor, and Sharon Neal, our proofreader, who worked diligently on the manuscript in order to bring it to its highest level of excellence.

And to each writer who contributed a part of yourselves, offering your personal stories, recipes, advice, and much more to give this book the heartfelt warmth and personal touch that we were searching for. We are so grateful!

We would also like to thank the readers of *The Godly Business Woman Magazine* for their priceless feedback that ultimately allowed us to see the need for such an endeavor. Educating, inspiring, and encouraging the workingwoman to maintain balance in her life is the reason we wanted to create *The Godly Business Woman Guide to Cooking and Entertainment.* We pray this book will help all women learn how to share the love of Jesus—professionally and at home.

And finally, we want to thank God for the partnership that he has given us. Together, we have the same desire to honor and glorify God and the same motivation to further his kingdom. We continually see God's hand in our alliance, moving us in the same direction and allowing us to work together toward the same goals. What a blessing it is to have a partnership that has transformed into a godly friendship—one that ultimately allows us to give our best to honor the Lord.

"We always thank God for all of you, mentioning you in our prayers" (1 Thess. 1:2).

Preface

THE GODLY BUSINESS WOMAN *Guide to Cooking and Entertainment* is a spiritual guide for the workingwoman and provides a resource for maintaining balance in her life. As Christian women, balance seems to be the number one concern of our busy lives. We get involved in more "things" but spend less time with God. How can we expect success?

To help you in your pursuit of godly living and entertaining, you must first and foremost focus on God. "Very early in the morning, while it was still dark, Jesus got up, left the house and went off to a solitary place, where he prayed" (Mark 1:35). Our first priority should always be to put God at the center of everything we do. Finding quiet time for prayer allows you to maintain that focus, and by getting in His Word each day, you will be able to find the success that God has planned for you.

The Godly Business Woman Guide to Cooking and Entertainment is a collection of stories and hands-on information that was specifically written to educate, inspire, and ultimately motivate godly businesswomen in effectively reaching out to others through entertaining.

In this book we want to show you how you can entertain in a variety of ways and still be able to minister to your family, friends, and coworkers. Whether you're young or old, married or single, a stay-at-home mom, or you work in a corporate environment, godly entertaining is something you can do. We'll give you the vital information necessary in planning, organizing, executing, and hosting such events as

- breakfasts and brunches,
- engagement parties,
- baby showers,
- children's parties, and
- holidays and festivals.

We are excited about sharing the information in this book, and we truly hope that God will use *The Godly Business Woman Guide to Cooking and Entertainment* to bless your life as much as it has blessed ours.

Section One
ENTERTAINING

We Didn't Know Evangelism Could Be Fun

VONETTE BRIGHT

NOT LONG AGO, my dear friend Lois Eger wrote a birthday poem and called me a "party girl." It's true! I love a party. I like getting people together—not only for fun, but also for a purpose. I like to see people enjoy themselves, relax, laugh, develop friendships, feel important and loved, and most of all, to be introduced to Jesus Christ. When they are blessed, I always feel rewarded. And I've discovered that one of the most effective ways to reach out to others is through joyful hospitality in our homes, in our neighborhoods, and where we work and play.

Everyone likes a party. Mention the word and eyes light up—any excuse to dress up or just get together with friends, neighbors, coworkers, and loved ones.

But many Christians don't know how to reach out. They worry about the high cost of entertaining or fear the responsibility of planning and hosting an event. Yet God honors all kinds of hospitality. "Therefore, my dear brothers, stand firm. Let nothing move you. Always give yourselves fully to the work of the Lord, because you know that your labor in the Lord is not in vain" (1 Cor. 15:58).

Paul makes it clear—God will honor your desires and efforts to honor Him. Whether you're a party girl or not, your hard work will not be in vain. Dinners for a few guests or for hundreds, lively children's parties, formal wedding receptions, company picnics, or afternoon teas are all effective ways to share the love of Christ.

Godly "Busy" Women

The idea for *The Godly Business Woman Guide to Cooking and Entertainment* came out of a desire to help these women. If you think about it, all women are businesswomen. The Proverbs (31:10–31) "ideal" woman had great wisdom, compassion, and character. She also had wonderful abilities—including being an excellent wife, mother, friend, and businesswoman—"her lamp does not go out at night" (she is busy). We, the authors of these collections, want to present simple, hands-on ideas to help you, the "busy" woman, host events and special occasions where you live and work. Our desire is to show you how to share your spiritual life through hosting everyday events, to educate and inspire you, as godly businesswomen.

Jesus said, "I no longer call you servants, because a servant does not know his master's business. Instead, I have called you friends, for everything that I learned from my Father I have made known to you" (John 15:15). As Christians, our mission is to share the friendship we have with Jesus with those who don't know Him personally and then help them begin to grow in their new faith. How does that start? Well, as mothers, we are to raise godly offspring; as friends, sisters, and daughters, we are to reach other friends and family; and as women in the workforce, we are to minister to everyone, executives, coworkers, employees, and customers—everyone with which we come in contact. No matter what our schedules look like or how hectic our lives seem, we are to exemplify Christ by being a lighthouse, not only in our home, but also at our job, in our city, state, and nation.

I began at an early age to see how rewarding entertaining and a life of sharing can be. When I was growing up, Mother and Dad loved to invite friends into our home. Some of my earliest recollections are of Mother teaching me to pass out napkins, to wait to be served last, and to pay attention to details that make guests feel comfortable and appreciated.

In those days, the population of Coweta, Oklahoma, our little town, was only 1,500, but we enjoyed an amazing number of formal events. Several professional couples had moved to the community, and our town enjoyed preserving some of the culture those people brought with them.

As a child, I observed afternoon teas and candlelighted dinners. As a teenager, I enjoyed formal parties and looked forward to the ice cream socials and watermelon feeds held by churches and various groups in the summer. Hayrides and barbecues brightened my winters. I was so impressed with these events that I thought, *It'll be so much fun to go to these parties when I'm grown up.*

Home and hospitality were so important to me that I chose to major in home economics in college. At the time, I didn't know how God would use the things I was learning. In fact, I wasn't even sure I was a Christian. Of course, God knew all about me and about the plans He had for my life.

By the time Bill Bright and I were married, the formal entertaining in Coweta had largely subsided. One exception was at my bridal shower. Every woman in town was invited. The hostesses asked me to wear a formal, and some of the other guests did, too. What a great time we had. Through this event and others, Bill and I saw how a home could be used to encourage people, so we wanted God to use ours to bless and enrich the lives of others.

Our Contract

During our second year of marriage, Bill suggested that we sign a contract with God, totally surrendering our lives to Him. Since Bill had signed hundreds of contracts as a businessman, an agreement between the Lord and us seemed reasonable to him.

"Let's write down exactly what we want out of life—our lifetime goals," Bill suggested, "to remind us that we are committed to working together." I agreed. Later that afternoon, we wrote and signed a contract, surrendering our lives completely and irrevocably to the Lord and to each other. That contract has formed the basis of our lives and ministry.

We listed everything we wanted out of this new life. Bill headed his list with "to be a slave of Jesus Christ." My list was more materialistic. (Wouldn't you know!) I wanted a home modest enough to invite a person from skid row (which was part of our ministry at that time) but lovely enough to entertain the president of the United States. That was a tall order.

Initial Attempts

We held our first modest dinner on March 17, 1949. Bill had met a businessman who didn't know Christ and invited the man and his wife to be our guests. But I had a problem. After our wedding on December 30, we left for California and honeymooned on the way. Immediately after we arrived in Los Angeles, I accepted a teaching position in the city school district and had just enough time to unpack before starting my new job. Now, just a few short weeks later, we were going to entertain in our new home.

I had much to learn about what God expects for hospitality. This was my first lesson. As wedding gift suggestions, I had chosen Lenox china, Bavarian crystal, and sterling silver. Bill and I had received generous wedding presents, but not enough to complete place settings for four. I *had* received twelve place settings of green glass dishes like those found inside boxes of oatmeal. I soon learned to appreciate that set of "twelve of everything."

I was elated that my dinner was scheduled on Saint Patrick's Day. How appropriate that we had green china. I placed a white cloth on the table, cut shamrocks from green construction paper for place mats, and used a Saint Patrick's Day theme in the centerpiece.

We spent the evening sharing our faith with the businessman and his wife. And I began to understand how to use what we had to honor Christ. God is gracious. He places no value on our possessions. He doesn't pressure us to perform, or require us to be sophisticated. Instead, He sees our hearts and understands our needs. Through the power of His Holy Spirit, He uses us where we live to help heal the hurts and broken spirits of those who need His love.

I'm so glad the Lord doesn't prefer the rich and famous or consider the poor person more worthy. He loves us as we are, then gives us the power to grow and serve Him with fruitful, holy lives. Relying on His strength and wisdom, I learned confidence in entertaining in a way that glorifies Him.

Special Guest

That simple dinner was just the beginning of a ministry for me. In the fall, Bill and I became involved in the 1949 Billy Graham Los Angeles Crusade. At the beginning of the several-week crusade, Bill said, "Vonette, I'm impressed by how you make people feel comfortable in our home. Would it be all right if I invited Billy Graham to dinner?"

My first thought was, *My oatmeal china.* "Could we buy another set of dishes?" I asked timidly.

Bill laughed. "Sounds like a good idea."

When Billy Graham accepted, Bill and I were excited about entertaining him and naive about what that meant. We bought Franciscan pottery from an outlet store. The set was gray and maroon and didn't match anything we had. The plates were so huge that they required an exorbitant amount of food to fill them.

But God's plan was not for a formal, silver-and-candles meal with me presiding as an elegant hostess. Instead, He arranged just the right kind of atmosphere for a special guest.

At that time, our home was a small two-bedroom English cottage at the back of a larger house in the Hollywood hills. The cottage had a lot of charm, but now I realize that it was not what most people would consider appropriate for entertaining the president of the United States—or Billy Graham.

Bill and I anticipated serving a small party, including Billy and an assistant or two, after the meeting. I stayed home that night to finish preparing the meal while Bill attended the service. When he returned, he brought Billy's entire team—Cliff Barrows, Grady and T. W. Wilson, George Beverly Shay, Jerry Bevins, Chuck Turner, George Wilson, and the organist and pianist—plus Stewart and Susie Hamlin.

Susie was a marvelous Christian woman who had been praying for her husband, a western radio entertainer. Stewart had not received Christ as his Savior, and she was thrilled that he had this opportunity to be with Billy Graham.

Susie realized my predicament and pitched in to help me prepare more food. Where it all came from, I'll never know. But we had plenty to eat—in spite of those huge plates. And Grady and T. W. Wilson's great jokes made the evening hilarious.

None of us forgot that meal. Certainly Stewart, whose business was storytelling, saw firsthand that the Christian life is not straight-laced, sober, or sad. A few days later, Stewart committed his life to Christ and gave his testimony at the crusade. I like to believe that our simple hospitality may have helped make a difference in his life.

Changing Lives

Does entertaining, whether at home with friends or at an office party with coworkers, intrigue you? You can experience fun and fellowship through many types of events, and oftentimes, just by living and setting a godly example, people come to know Christ. Godly living and entertaining not only grows us as individuals, but also spreads to those around us. As Christians, we have the privilege of building up the Kingdom—one event at a time. Now that's exciting!

VONETTE BRIGHT is the cofounder of Campus Crusade for Christ, mother, grandmother, discipler, speaker, and author. Her several books include *My Heart in His Hands, The Woman Within,* and *The Sister Circle,* which she coauthored with Nancy Moser. Bright is heard daily on the radio program "Women Today." Her greatest delight was being the life partner of Bill Bright for fifty-five years.

2

CHAPTER

Planning the Big Event

ELIZABETH STONE

PLANNING AN EVENT, no matter how large or small, can be a daunting task. Every successful event has a purpose and utilizes our gifts of hospitality and organization. As stated in 1 Peter 4: 9, God calls us to "Offer hospitality to one another without grumbling. Each one should use whatever gift he has received to serve others faithfully, administering God's grace in its various forms."

Events are a celebration of life. They are the creation of memories around special occasions such as birthdays, weddings, Christmas dinners, business functions, and friendly gatherings. Whether you're an experienced hostess or a first-time fearful planner, you'll want to consider purpose, logistics, and creation of an experience to put together a successful and grace-filled event.

Purpose: Why and Who

The first and most important step in planning a party is to determine its purpose. Why are you having an event? Are you entertaining new friends? Has your husband invited over his business partners and notified you at the last

---

THE EVENT BASICS AT A GLANCE

Why: The Reason for the Event

Who: Guests and Guest Count

Where: Location of the Event

When: The Date and the Time

What: Food, Beverages, Theme, Flowers, Decorations, Lighting, and Invitations

---

moment? Maybe it is your fortieth birthday or you want to impress your in-laws. Or, you just want to have a casual steak dinner on the grill with friends to catch up. Are you planning your daughter's wedding? Do you need to hire a caterer? Sometimes the reason is just to have a party, and that is okay. Whatever the reason, be sure to clearly define in your mind and preferably on paper why you're having a party. Keeping a journal or list for your event is a great tool. Completing this step will make all the other steps much easier.

Next, determine whom you will invite—family, friends, or business associates? You will need names, addresses, and maybe phone numbers. Start with a list of everyone whom you want to invite. Later in the planning process, you can determine if you need to reduce the size of your list, based on budgetary or location constraints.

Logistical Issues: Where and When

Now that you have decided the reason for your event and whom you want to attend, it is time to decide where to have the event. Make sure that your location enhances the reason for the event. You will want to consider the size, the availability, the ease of access, and the site's traffic pattern. Does the space work for the event's purpose? The home is without question the first choice for any entertaining. Whether it is a small intimate dinner or a backyard barbeque, the home creates the highest level of intimacy and hospitality. You can always choose a restaurant or other venue if your home is not appropriate for the event. Some interesting locations other than the home include gardens, museums, art galleries, offices, parks, or even boats.

Next, determine the type of event you will host. Will it be a breakfast, brunch, luncheon, afternoon tea, late-night dinner, formal seated dinner, casual Sunday night supper, or desserts after the theatre? Decide on a general time for the event, and then select a day and date. For example, you may want to have your event on June 15, a Saturday. If the date is flexible, carefully think about other conflicts that your guests might have. Conflicts could include holidays, vacations, children's activities, sporting or cultural events, or other social commitments. After the date is selected, choose an appropriate time. For example, on a Sunday night, you would want to start your event earlier, at 6 or 6:30 P.M., because it is a school night. People like to get home at a reasonable hour on Sundays and other weeknights. On a Saturday night, you can start later, say 7:30 or 8 P.M. On Friday nights, the preference is to start a little later to give your guests time to get home from work and get refreshed.

For the final step of the logistical stage, the formality of the event must be decided. Is this a black-tie affair such as a twenty-fifth wedding anniversary where you will want to have servers to wait on your guests, or is this a meet-and-greet casual gathering in your home? Business gatherings can be coat and tie, or business casual. Maybe you're having a themed event such as celebrating the Chinese New Year or a Mexican party. The event's formality will determine the style and the type of dress you will request from your guests.

The budget—oh, that budget. It is important to decide what the budget will be for your event. Spend your money wisely. Put the most dollars into your food costs.

Creating the Experience: the Senses

Now the fun begins. Allow your creativity and unique style to flow. Think about all of the senses: sight, smell, taste, hearing, and touch. By including

---

THE SENSES THAT CREATE THE EXPERIENCE

Sight: Invitations, Lights, Color, and Flowers

Hearing: Music

Smell: Flowers, Food, and Candles

Taste: Food and Beverages

Touch: Linens, Tablecloths and Napkins

---

all of the senses in your planning, you will enhance your guests' overall experience. Remember, the idea is to create a memorable experience of hospitality.

Sight

From the theme to the invitation, the décor, the flowers, and the lighting, the visual impact is critical. The theme and invitation set the tone. The décor creates the mood. The lighting produces the drama, and the color emphasizes the style. All of these sound very expensive, but none has to be. The invitations can be hand drawn or done on the computer. The flowers can be small glasses of different sizes and colors filled with a variety of individual flowers. You can put a grouping of three to four small vases in the middle of your table—and make sure that you can see over the vases or centerpiece so that your guests can speak to one another. Lighting can be created by turning off all the regular lights and using candlelight or by dimming your own lights.

Create an idea and let it flow throughout the event. For a Mardi Gras–themed event, hand deliver a mask with each invitation, and ask the guest to wear it to the party. Let strips of purple, green, and yellow craft paper serve as your tablecloth. Put Mardi Gras beads on the tables. Add crayons in purple, yellow, and green. Play a little New Orleans jazz music. Fix a specialty drink of the evening and serve Cajun cuisine.

Hearing

Whether it is a band, a DJ, or a CD, music helps to create the experience. Choose lighter or softer music in the earlier parts of the event. Then move to more energetic and louder music. Decide whether the music is a primary function of the event, as it would be if dancing were involved, or if the music will be in the background for ambiance.

Smell

Beautiful aromas can be created with flowers, herbs, and candles. It is important to use soft aromas so as not to overpower the food. The food in and of itself must smell wonderful. If the food looks great and smells great, then you know it will taste wonderful. Lavender and rosemary are both wonderful aromas that work well with foods.

Taste

Select foods that enhance your overall vision for the occasion. For an Italian-themed event, why not serve good old-fashioned spaghetti and meatballs with buttery garlic bread? Or make Osso Bucco, a delicious and more formal Italian dish. Remember to revisit your purpose when planning the menu. Food does not have to be elaborate to be wonderful. Sometimes, the best and most memorable meals are the ones that are very simple. The most important part of cooking is to use good ingredients. Do not skimp in this area. There is an old saying that a little butter is good and a lot of butter is better.

Beverages also should reflect the tone of your event. For hot dogs and hamburgers on the grill, offer iced tea and cold beverages. For something more elegant, offer a wider selection of beverages along with nice wines during the dinner. To add to the fun, create a specialty beverage of the evening. Some specialty beverage ideas* might include a "Mango Margarita" for a

_____

*Specialty beverages should not be considered synonymous with alcohol; these and other drinks can be made without alcohol as well.

tropical event or an "Azalea Punch" for a spring event when the azaleas are in bloom. Drinks such as "Mojitos" and "Sangria" are also popular specialty drinks that work very well with Spanish food.

Touch

Everything your guests will touch—the napkins, the glasses, the tablecloths, and the silverware—has a part in creating the experience. Tablecloths and napkins can be paper or cotton, damask or silk. The feel of the napkins and the silverware and glassware all embellish the experience.

Special Touches

Add a special touch to your event to make it more memorable. Offer a take-home gift for your guests, maybe some chocolates or a gift handmade by your children. Give the guests a bundle of herbs tied with beautiful ribbon when they walk in the door. Small intimate touches can truly personalize an event.

Create avenues for conversation. Instead of one long dinner buffet, have smaller buffets or stations around your home or the event site. This creates traffic flow and conversation. Use a conversation icebreaker, especially in situations where the guests do not know each other. One technique is to put on name tags the names of famous couples in history, such as Fred and Wilma Flintstone, Ronald and Nancy Reagan, or Fred Astaire and Ginger Rogers. As your guests walk in the door, put a name tag on the back of each guest and tell him or her to walk around the room asking other guests only yes and no questions to find out the name. Once a guest figures out who he or she is, it's time to find the other half of the couple and sit with that person at dinner. It's a great way to get an evening—and all kinds of conversations—started.

Always think about the flow and progression of the event. Eliminate traffic jams by putting beverage stations away from the front door and desserts in another room away from the main dining area. Guests can have one course or hors d'oeuvres in one area and then move to another area for dining. Serve dessert in a third area. This keeps the event's energy high.

An Example of an Event that Tantalizes the Senses

Purpose:
Volunteer Appreciation Dinner for a Christian Nonprofit

Logistics:
Two hundred guests
Event venue in a central location
Tuesday evening in October
6:30 P.M.
Dress: Business Attire

Creating the Experience:
Theme—The Fruit of the Spirit (Galatians 5:22)

Invitation—Simple card with a band of fruits around the edges in fall colors

Color—Centerpieces and tablecloths in rich reds, oranges, and corals

Lighting—Lights in the room dimmed very low and votive candles on each table

Music—Trio playing softly in the background

Food—Five-course elegant seated dinner, each course by a different Christian chef

Centerpieces:
Bountiful bowls of autumn fruits

Added Special Touches:
Each chef reads a Scripture verse when announcing the course. Guests are given gourmet candied apples wrapped in cellophane as gifts. Instead of using table numbers, each table is given the name of a fruit. The guests are given a card with a fruit name on it to determine the table at which they are to be seated.

Remember, God is in the details and the details create the experience. A truly great party is an experience to remember. It will expand your imagination and embellish your senses.

Entertaining should be fun. Use your skills, your talents, and your imagination. You don't have to spend a lot of money to have a great event. The most important part is the planning and organization. If you love to cook, then do so. If not, hire a caterer or get the food from a restaurant. If you're hosting a large event, hire an event planner. Be a confident and cheerful hostess. Put your trust in God. He is with you and will guide and encourage you as you fulfill His wishes to offer hospitality and administer His grace.

ELIZABETH STONE is President and CEO of The Stone Kitchen Catering and Special Events, Houston's leading catering company. She is a graduate of Southern Methodist University and self-taught in the culinary field. For fifteen years, the impetus behind the company's phenomenal success is passion and commitment to excellence. The company embraces that God is in the details.

Menus to Remember

JOE BOWDEN, PH.D.

REMEMBER HOW MUCH you disliked busywork in school? The same is true when you're trying to plan a party to remember. Follow the KISS principle—keep it sanely simple.

If you try to have too many details in your plan—too much busywork—you won't enjoy the event. You'll be worrying about what you forgot to do and wondering if your guests noticed your mistakes. They may not notice your mistakes—but they will notice that you're nervous and distracted.

As you're planning, try to maintain focus on what your guests will remember (or "take home" with them) when they leave. One word to keep in mind is *conversation*. Conversation is the central activity of all events, whether casual or formal. God created us for fellowship and conversation, and when you plan for fellowship, each aspect of the event will, in one way or another, be centered around it. "For where two or three come together in my name, there am I with them" (Matt. 18:20). From icebreaker to dessert, planning can keep God at your table. Even after-meal activities like coffee, games, a video, or just relaxing can stimulate deeper conversations and fellowship.

To set the scene and determine just how sanely simple and enjoyable this will be, ask yourself these questions:

1. What's the occasion? Is it a casual luncheon, office Christmas party, or intimate dinner?
2. Who's invited? Friends, family, coworkers, neighbors, prospective clients, or new church members?
3. How will you serve the meal? Does the occasion merit a sit-down formal dinner, or would a buffet work?
4. What will you serve? If many of your guests are on one of the high-protein/low-carbohydrate diets, lay off the fancy breads and candied desserts. If there is a possibility that some could be vegetarian or diabetic, be sure to consider their dietary restrictions. And just as important: serve something you have served before. This just puts your mind at ease—why have to worry about whether your menu will look like the picture in the book, let alone taste right? Remember, keep it sanely simple.

Menus can be very simple or elegant all with the same food items. The difference is the time required for presentation and amount of detail to which you wish to attend. With preparation, each dish will be ready for you to serve without a lot of time away from your guests.

We're going to show you five different, well-balanced menus that can be served four or more ways to create a meal you and your guests are sure to remember. This collection can help you plan more than twenty different occasions.

One final reminder, Jesus told us in the story of Mary and Martha (see Luke 10:38) that it is better to spend time at His feet than in the kitchen. When in doubt, plan a simpler menu. Spend the time you save with Jesus and your guests will surely walk away with a memory that will last a lifetime.

The basic planning process of any menu is its presentation, which should be fun and memorable.

〜 Menus to Remember

Example 1: A Basic Meat, Vegetable, and Potatoes Menu

Appetizer/salad: Fresh vegetables and fruit
Main meat dish: Spiced ham [spiral cut or regular butt cut]
Vegetable: Steamed and buttered
Potatoes and bread
Dessert: Strawberry caramel cheesecake

This simple menu can be served as a cold buffet, a hot buffet, a casual dinner, and a formal dinner. The key is how they are served. The following will show how to start simple and move to a more elegant approach. We will take some time to demonstrate this selection in all formats. The other four menus will be in your capable hands—with an additional hint or two.

APPETIZER/SALAD

Hot and Cold Buffets—Serve a salad or finger food with dips and dressings [herb dip/ranch dressing] arranged on white or brightly colored platters with garnish [parsley, mint, red lettuce, or fresh-cut flowers].

Casual Dinner—Assemble the vegetables and fruit into a colorful salad in a bowl matching your table service. Garnish the bowl with orange slices, large stuffed olives, radish slices, and small button mushrooms and serve with a choice of dressings.

Formal Dinner—Make each salad up on its plate, cover with plastic film and keep cool until served. Start with a leaf or two of red lettuce, mixed greens with broccoli, mini carrots, tomato wedges, two or three cold steamed asparagus

---

The only difference between a casual event and a formal dinner is often only in the presentation. The menus can be the same.

spears tied near the bottom with a strip of pimiento or thin sliced red bell pepper, garnished on one side with a thin orange slice, whole fresh strawberry, and two or three small white mushrooms. Again, have a choice of dressings.

MAIN MEAT DISH

Cold Buffet—Precook ham and serve cold, cut from the bone, or use deli ham varieties. Garnish the serving platter with sliced pineapple and red maraschino cherries or fresh strawberries. *Tip:* Remember, a garnish is not a food group so please use your KISS principle.

Hot Buffet—Serve the ham hot, garnished as above.

Casual Dinner—Bake the ham with a garnish of whole cloves punched into the ham slices, a sprinkle of brown sugar over the ham and serve on a heated platter at the head of the table; carve and serve.

Formal Dinner—Bake ham as above, cut into slices and trim excess fat. Place the slices on a serving platter in a half-moon shape and sprinkle a small amount of brown sugar down the middle of the arrangement. Fill the hollow of the shape with pineapple and maraschino cherries, keep hot, and just before serving, garnish midline of meat slices with fresh mint or rosemary sprigs/leaves.

VEGETABLE

Cold Buffet—Use a second platter of different vegetables arranged in colorful patterns. This platter can have pickled mushrooms, stuffed olives, blanched asparagus, sliced squash, etc. With this plate, have different dips and dressings [French onion dip/blue cheese dressing].

Hot Buffet—Steam or bake an assortment of vegetables and toss in a hot pan with herb butter and serve in a hot chafing dish.

Casual Dinner—Use the same vegetables as above except serve in hot dishes and garnish with red bell pepper/onion circles, parsley sprigs, or a circle of baked herb croutons.

Formal Dinner—Arrange the vegetables by groups on a longer serving dish. For example, arrange asparagus, long green beans, yellow squash, and green zucchini strips. Mini carrots and snow pea pods can be mixed with thin circles of red, green, and yellow pepper, and a bit of parsley will finish the tray.

POTATOES AND BREAD

Cold Buffets—Select various potato chips or potato salads garnished with egg slices and parsley. Use a variety of breads, including mixed rolls, Kaiser, etc.

Hot Buffets—Use small steamed red potatoes, buttered and garnished with fresh ground pepper and parsley. Use hot herb breads/rolls.

Casual Dinner—Serve the same steamed red potatoes as in the hot buffet, except serve bread with herb butter or herb olive oil for dipping. In the dinner setting, the bread can be served first with the salad and replenished as needed.

Formal Dinner—Bake both round, smooth-skinned white potatoes and sweet potatoes until done. Cut the white potatoes in half and carefully clean out and mash; mix with bits of green onion and bacon. Peel and mash the sweet potatoes. Mix with drained crushed pineapple, sour cream, and a bit of brown sugar. Fill half of the white potato skin with white potato mixture and half with sweet potato mixture. Sprinkle with dry parsley and bake a second time. Add colorful garnishes and serve hot. Use the same breads as those used with the casual dinner.

DESSERT

Hot and Cold Buffets—Cut plain cheesecake into one-inch squares, arrange about one-half inch apart on a simple, white serving dish. Pour your favorite sweetened pie filling to cover all of the squares. Top each square with a small amount of whipped topping and a thin slice of strawberry, a cherry, or other fresh berry to match your topping. Serve chilled.

Casual and Formal Dinners—First swirl a bit of caramel syrup/topping on a dessert plate, then a swirl of strawberry syrup. Cut the cheesecake into one- to two-inch slices, place on its side on the swirls. Top with a spoonful

> A few minutes of planning will cure an hour of wasted haste.

of pie filling, a bit of whipped topping, fresh berries [just a few] to match the filling, a dark chocolate curl, and a fresh mint leaf alongside and serve chilled.

For each of these menus, the cooking and preparation time is about the same. Each is taken from casual to elegant with a bit more imagination, color and flair. For instance, in the menu above, you could substitute a beef roast, pork roast, leg of lamb or a rolled turkey roast and, with minor changes in the garnishes, each would be fit for a king.

When your guests enter your home, they should feel welcome. Something as simple as the aroma of a batch of fresh baked cookies from a ready-to-bake package, mulling cider, or simple aromatic candles will win over your guests before they even sit down. Remember not to combine too many aromas in your menu—garlic bread and mulled cider don't mix very well. One tells us of hearty Italian dishes and the other of quiet evenings in the fall or winter.

Now that you have your feet wet, let your creative juices work around our other four simple menus. Bear in mind that each menu can be served casual to elegant—just allow more planning for the presentation, and don't forget, keep the time away from your guests at an absolute minimum.

Example 2: A Basic Southwestern Menu

APPETIZER/SALAD

Hot and Cold Buffets—Display mixed colored tortilla chips and red & green chunky salsa, hot or cold cheese dip [con quesa], and bean dip in colorful dishes. Spread a soft flour tortilla with soft cream cheese, sprinkle with chopped green chilies, roll and cut into one-half-inch spirals, and serve cold.

Casual and Formal Dinners—Mix a green salad with rings of red, yellow, and green bell peppers, red onion, then garnish with mild cherry peppers, garlic croutons, and fresh cilantro. Serve with lime cilantro dressing. Can also use the cream cheese spirals with the casual dinner.

MAIN MEAT DISH/VEGETABLE

Hot and Cold Buffets—Serve crisp mini tacos, soft shell tacos, black bean salad with corn, green onion, and chopped colored peppers marinated in oil, lime juice, and a touch of chile oil or pepper sauce.

MAIN MEAT DISH/VEGETABLE/BREAD

Casual and Formal Dinners—Serve platters of mixed enchiladas with tamales or breaded chicken breasts stuffed with white pepper cheese, topped with sliced avocado and a small cherry pepper. Serve with green chili chicken or pork sauce and mixed pinto and black beans. Serve with hot tortillas, honey, and butter. For formal dinners, be creative; use garnishes, colorful dishes, and bright napkins—color.

DESSERT

Use for All Settings—Serve vanilla ice cream or flan pudding with strips of buttered baked pie crust, topped with brown sugar, cinnamon, and a touch of nutmeg. For a formal setting, place two or three baked strips in a small dish with ice cream garnish with mint leaves and red and green cherries.

Example 3: A Basic Chicken Strip Menu

APPETIZER/SALAD

Hot and Cold Buffets—Create a mixed green salad with sliced colorful vegetables, cheese, and croutons, topped with thinly sliced spiced chicken strips grilled and served with mixed crackers and a variety of cream cheese spreads [veggie, fruit, chives, etc.].

Casual and Formal Dinners—Use the same as for buffets except dress up the presentation with grape tomatoes, sliced avocado, and circles of thin-sliced red onion. Omit chicken strips and cheese; serve with fresh baked bread sticks and herb butter.

MAIN MEAT DISH/VEGETABLE

Hot and Cold Buffets—Use quick kabobs. Cut chicken strips into one-inch chunks, brown lightly with a bit of brown sugar. On wooden skewers, thread one-inch chunks of red onion, colored bell pepper, cherry tomatoes, and pineapple chunks; serve hot over a bed of quick cook brown rice.

Hot or Cold Casserole—Cut strips into thin slices, brown with slivered onion, and mix can of cheddar cheese soup, one can of milk, one can of water and one and a half cups of instant rice; mix well and bake until rice is done, top with cheese, and serve hot or cold.

Casual and Formal Dinners—Steam or microwave mixed vegetables tossed with chopped salted cashews and capers.

Prepare creamed chicken strips [cut diagonal], sautéed button mushrooms and steamed asparagus [cut in two-inch sections] and serve over wild/brown rice garnished with mint leaves and thin strips of pimiento.

For a casual dinner, serve hot chicken casserole described above, except add croutons before baking.

DESSERT

Use for All Settings—Two-inch squares of baked brownies [soft] can be set on a small plate dusted with powdered sugar and drizzled with chocolate syrup. Serve with glazed cherries and curls of dark chocolate topped with whipped cream.

Example 4: A Basic Fish [Salmon] Menu

APPETIZER/SALAD

Hot and Cold Buffets—A platter of mixed vegetables and cheeses with crab dip can be served with your favorite salad.

MAIN MEAT DISH/VEGETABLE/BREAD

Hot and Cold Buffets—First bake/broil a full salmon filet brushed with oil and topped with fresh chopped basil and serve hot or cold. If cold, cut into one-half-inch squares and serve with mixed crackers and mini bagels and a variety of cream cheese spreads. A cold tuna dish of mini pasta or angel hair pasta, drained tuna, finely chopped green onion, celery, a bit of fresh pepper, and mixed with salad dressing or light mayo will round out the buffet. If hot, cut salmon diagonally in one-inch slices, garnish with fresh basil, and serve with steamed vegetables mixed with small red potatoes and hot bread. Can also serve cold or hot steamed shrimp and cocktail sauce. [Always use fresh seafood to avoid a fishy smell.]

APPETIZER/SALAD

Casual and Formal Dinners—Serve cold shrimp cocktail [deveined please] with sauce and also your favorite green salad dressed up and colorful.

MAIN MEAT DISH/VEGETABLE/BREAD

Casual and Formal Dinners—Casual or formal will use the same selection as the hot buffet except serve with garnishes, heated serving dishes. Use two- to three-inch salmon filets, brushed with olive oil, a bit of fresh pepper, and fresh chopped basil; grill or bake and serve on a bed of red lettuce leaves, garnish with black olives and blanched almonds. Toss a medley of steamed vegetables in hot olive oil or lemon butter and serve over steaming rice pilaf.

DESSERT

Use for All Settings—Fill small dishes with cut fresh fruit mixed with orange juice, small marshmallows, coconut, and pecan halves. Top with a scoop of fruit sherbet.

Example 5: A Basic Vegetarian Menu

The key to a vegetarian menu is to watch out for too much carbohydrate and too little protein.

APPETIZER/SALAD/SOUP/MAIN DISH/DESSERT

Hot and Cold Buffets—Serve a hearty twelve-bean soup with green chilies added for a kick [for more protein add tofu]. This can be served hot or cold. Arrange platters of mixed vegetables, sliced avocado [dip in orange or lime juice to maintain color], cheeses, and fruit with a selection of dips. Mixed nuts or bowls of different nuts for a variety and a selection of cream cheese spreads with breads, bagels, crackers, and a selection of juices will top off the buffet, hot or cold. For dessert, serve mixed fruit sherbets and/or pineapple upside-down cake cut into small squares.

Casual and Formal Dinners—For the casual or formal setting, bake small acorn squash. Cut in half, clean, brush with olive oil, and stuff with a mixture of chopped apple, pineapple, walnuts, and croutons; cover with foil and bake; serve hot. Provide a hearty green salad with cashews, herb bread sticks, and a variety of dressings. Steam layered vegetables and small potatoes, lightly butter, mix with green capers, and serve on a layer of wild rice/brown rice with colorful garnish. For dessert, prepare baked apples stuffed with a bit of brown sugar, maraschino cherries, pineapple, and pecans; serve hot and top with a bit of coconut and heavy cream or ice cream.

DESSERT

Casual or Formal Dinner—Pineapple upside-down cake: Place on serving dish [one full pineapple slice per serving] and be sure to have red cherries baked in the center of the slice. Top with whipped cream and a light dusting of nutmeg and a mint leaf.

As in the kitchen, where a sharp knife is a tool in your hand, a prepared hostess is a tool in God's hand. Listen to His guidance and you will be able to present your occasion as a praise offering.

JOE BOWDEN, PH.D., a research biochemist, teacher, and inventor, loves cooking, storytelling, and children. He and his wife, Elaine, share a love of writing and painting. Current projects include a collection of poetry, a mystery novel series for boys, and an ongoing newsletter for writers. Joe and Elaine have shared forty-two years together and have two grown children and two grandchildren.

Basic Etiquette for All Occasions

Jill Rigby

SARAH WILLIS, better known as Fanny Fern, educated her nineteenth-century American readers in etiquette and the need for "punctiliousness" in *Fern Leaves from Fanny's Portfolio.* Mrs. Willis's book published in 1853 sold nearly 100,000 copies, making it the best seller of the year.

In 1896, Dorothy Dix wrote the first syndicated etiquette column in the *New Orleans Picayune,* giving detailed instructions in all areas of domestic and

---

Punctiliousness sounds like a word from *Mary Poppins*, doesn't it? *Merriam-Webster* shows that punctilious originated in 1637, meaning "a concern about the precise accordance with the details of codes or conventions." Certainly, we could all be a bit more punctilious today.

---

social life. She had quite a way of making her point: "If we told our friends as plainly of their faults as we do the partners of our bosom, we wouldn't have an acquaintance left who would speak to us. If, when we are invited out to dinner, we criticize the cooking as freely as we do the home table, we should never be asked a second time. If, when we go out to other people's homes we made as little effort to be agreeable and entertaining as we do in our own, our invitations would be as scarce as hen's teeth."

It doesn't take much to see why both genders found her words unsettling, but nonetheless true. She was known for her blunt directness in promoting politeness.

But my personal favorite, Mrs. Edith B. Ordway, in 1913 published a wonderful little book, *Etiquette of To-Day*. Her writings expanded the discussion of etiquette to the attitudes behind the actions. Her book opens with these words: "Etiquette will not take the place of character, nor of accurate knowledge of human nature and the arts of practical life. Given these, however, it will unlock to any man or woman doors of success and profit and real happiness that, without it, would have remained forever closed. . . . Without unselfishness and a fine consideration for others, the art of etiquette would be impossible."

We know as women of the twenty-first century that these words still hold true. A working knowledge of etiquette will open doors when character is at the heart of the individual.

Long before our women writers, a gentleman by the name of Peter would be considered a master of etiquette with these words found in Scripture: "Offer hospitality to one another without grumbling. Each one should use whatever gift he has received to serve others, faithfully administering God's grace in its various forms. If anyone speaks, he should do it as one speaking the very words of God. If anyone serves, he should do it with the strength God provides, so that in all things God may be praised through Jesus Christ" (1 Pet. 4:9–11).

Take it from our experts: entertaining is a way to serve your guests and family with warm hospitality from a heart filled with God's grace and love.

Remember to do unto others as you would have others do unto you. When you receive an invitation, pick up the phone or fill in the reply card when you receive it. Our own good intentions to RSVP sometimes are forgotten in our busy days.

Entertaining Etiquette and Everyday Manners

Invitations

The invitation should set the tone for the gathering and include the five W's: Who, What, Where, When, and Why. But the most important information for your guests' comfort is the suggested attire. These days, it's often difficult to discern the proper dress from the style of invitation. Stick to the basics: "Casual, no jeans" or "Dressy" or, if you want an elegant affair, "After five." (I would love to ask the person who coined the phrase "dress casual" what she had in mind.)

Don't feel that you're being "bossy" by stating beginning and ending times. Guests are more comfortable when they know the time frame the host has in mind.

To RSVP or not to RSVP, that is the question. Unfortunately, in today's world, few people respond to this request. If you don't feel comfortable estimating the number of guests who will attend, it is appropriate to make a call the week before the event to find an accurate guest count.

Addressing Invitations

Use the list below as a reference when addressing invitations:

Married couple:	Mr. and Mrs. Jonathan Bridgewater
Married couple, physician husband:	Dr. and Mrs. Thomas Edwards
Married couple, physician wife:	Mr. and Mrs. Stafford Kendall or
	Dr. Emily Kendall and Mr. Stafford Kendall

Married couple, both physicians:	The Doctors Williams or Dr. John Williams and Dr. Sarah Williams
Married couple, husband is a judge:	The Honorable and Mrs. Bob Downing
Married couple, wife is a judge:	The Honorable Laura Davis and Mr. Amos Davis
Single man:	Mr. John Rigby
Single woman:	Miss Helen Waites
Widow:	Mrs. Carl Jones
Divorced woman:	Mrs. Julie Wright
Divorced woman, resumed name:	Ms. Julie Smith
For children over 18 living at home, send a separate invitation or list their names below their parents:	Mr. and Mrs. Jonathan Bridgewater Miss Sally Bridgewater Mr. John Bridgewater
For children under 18:	Mr. and Mrs. Jonathan Bridgewater and family

Note: Titles such as Reverend, Captain, Lieutenant, Rabbi, and so on should not be abbreviated.

Invitations should be sent two to three weeks in advance of a home celebration. During the holidays, your guests would appreciate three weeks' notice. Invitations to catered parties or large events should be sent four weeks in advance to give you enough time to prepare for the anticipated number of guests.

Hospitable Hostess

Picture this hospitable hostess found in 1 Timothy 5:10, "She is well known for her good deeds, such as bringing up children, showing hospitality, washing the feet of the saints, helping those in trouble and devoting herself to all kinds of good deeds." Hospitality comes from the Greek word *philocenia,* which in its basic form means "to love."

One of my sons called me from the deer camp when he was eleven years old, panting so hard I could barely understand his words, "I got one, Mom. . . . It was great. . . . I did it all by myself. . . . We're coming home now for supper." Click!

Fortunately, the deer camp was an hour and a half from our home. A quick trip to the fabric store to pick up camp fabric set the mood at the supper table. I gathered all the hunting stuff left at our house to make a centerpiece. Broken branches became an imitation deer rack which I mounted in a soccer trophy covered with a cardboard plaque that read: WORLD'S BEST DEER HUNTER.

Within minutes of putting the final touches on the instant celebration, my little boy sashayed through the door, extending his hand for a handshake rather than a hug with the confidence of a grown man. When he saw the homemade trophy, he jumped in my arms and said, "Mom, you did this for me? I'm not the best, you are."

The secret to being a perfect hostess is loving your guests. Truly, with God's love. So, relax—love covers a multitude of mistakes. Here are a few suggestions to maximize your comfort and minimize your errors:

- When planning the menu, consider those with restricted diets. Offering a variety of side dishes—vegetables and salads—accommodates most needs.
- Have a special place for your pets separate from your guests during the event.
- If a guest asks to bring a friend to the party, it's up to you. You may have no objection. But you can politely say no, if you feel it is too much of an imposition.

- A successful hostess makes her guests feel special. As your company arrives, it is your responsibility to make introductions. Include an interesting fact about each person as you introduce him or her to one another. This helps break the ice and open the way for conversation to begin.
- Keep the party moving. If you serve light appetizers, don't keep your guests lingering too long for dinner.
- Don't hold dinner for late arrivals.
- If possible, separate the dinner from the dessert. Most desserts can be eaten without the benefit of a dining table. Move to another area of your home to enjoy the sweet after-dinner treat.
- Serve caffeinated and decaffeinated coffee.
- You set the end time for the party. It can be printed on the invitations, or you can gently comment how much you appreciate your guests spending the evening in your home and you're looking forward to seeing them again.
- If you receive a hostess gift, you need to acknowledge it with a handwritten note within a week of the party.

Grateful Guest

- RSVP, always, within three days of receiving the invitation. If you find that you can attend after declining, call immediately, offering the understanding that it may be too late to change the plans.
- Refrain from asking to bring extra guests, unless it is a family situation or true necessity.
- Arrive on time. Forty-five minutes early is just as inconsiderate as forty-five minutes late. I recently hosted an eight o'clock breakfast meeting in my office. I was dismayed when a young woman arrived at 7:15. I apologized that I couldn't stop at the moment to talk because I was finishing last-minute preparations. She said, "Oh, I understand, I'll just have a glass of juice." I turned to point her in the direction of the beverage table when she added, "I'll take ice with my

juice." She took a seat at the conference table to gather her thoughts while I poured her juice and went back to the kitchen for ice.

- Turn off your cell phone when you enter someone's home. You can excuse yourself during the party to call home and check with the babysitter.
- It's a sweet gesture to bring a small hostess gift—a box of candy, bath soaps, etc. Just keep it simple. It's meant to be a token of appreciation.
- Help the hostess by introducing yourself to other guests. Be an engaging listener.
- Watch your hostess for clues to begin eating.
- Don't smoke without asking.
- Offer to help clean up, but do not insist.
- Don't make a habit of being the last one to leave.
- Thank your hostess before you leave.
- Send a short note of thanks within a week of the event.

MY FAVORITE ENTERTAINING? FEEDING A BUNCH OF TEENAGE GUYS

Our house was the "hangout" when our twin sons were in high school. I loved to hear the cars pull up the driveway at midnight on Fridays. The ice cream came out of the freezer and I put brownies in the oven while heating the caramel sauce.

The guys came barreling in, opened the fridge door, grabbed a cold Coke and settled in to talk. I admit I spoiled them. Some nights they wanted eggs and toast. Other nights it was tacos and nachos. Our home became the refuge from the world. When Saturday morning came, I rolled out beignets and fried homemade sausage.

I always thought it was just the food that made our house popular during the high school years until a few months ago when I attended a formal event with my grown sons and their buddies. Much to my surprise, they told one story after another about nights at our house. Even more thrilling, I was asked to dance every dance. I guess it was more than the food that kept them coming back.

Manners at the Table

- You should allow twenty-four inches for each place setting at a dining table.
- An easy way to remember the order of the place setting is liquids on the right and solids on the left. Glasses, cups, saucers, knives, and spoons go on the right. Salad plates, bread and butter plates, napkins, and forks belong on the left.
- Elbows on the table are permissible between courses or after the plates have been cleared. You can rest your wrists on the table during dinner, if needed.
- Do not season your food before tasting it. That's insulting to your host.
- If your soup is too hot to eat, let it rest until cooled. Don't blow.
- Tear bite-size pieces of rolls and bread, buttering only one piece at a time. The exception is breakfast breads, such as biscuits and toast. Spread the whole piece so the butter can melt. Mmm, mmm good.
- Leave the table during the meal only if absolutely necessary. No explanation is needed; simply say, "Excuse me."
- Ask to have a condiment passed to you rather than reaching across someone's place setting.
- Use your knife only when a fork will not cut sufficiently. Always use a knife and fork to cut salad if the pieces are too large. Using a fork could result in lettuce flying through the air and landing in your neighbor's plate.
- Pass the salt and pepper together.
- If a piece of food falls from your plate, lift it with your silverware and place it on the edge of your plate.

Napkin Notes

- The most practical and sensible way to place a cloth napkin in your lap is to fold it by thirds, not in half. Place it on your lap with the folded edge toward your body. This allows you to blot your mouth without staining your clothing.

- If you must leave the table during the meal, place your napkin on your chair seat so others are not viewing soiled linen on the table.
- When the meal is finished, loosely fold your napkin and place it on the left of your place at the table.

Final Thoughts

God put a song in my heart when my twin sons entered first grade. For twelve years, my boys and their friends heard these words as their wake-up call if they were sleeping at our house:

> Oh, it's a bright and beautiful day
> God made it special that way.
> We're gonna sing and shout His name
> Hosanna, Praise His name.
> And if your day gets tough,
> Just remember to look above
> And Jesus will shine His love on you.
> I said, Jesus will shine His love on you,
> One more time . . .
> I said, Jesus will shine His love on you.
> Yes, He will!

About a dozen high school seniors were snoozing on the game room floor early one Saturday morning. Soccer practice was in an hour and breakfast was ready.

When I opened the door I just couldn't resist, "Oh, it's a bright and beautiful day . . ." as I knelt down to gently persuade these sleeping giants to rise and shine. My heart began to swell as one bass voice after another joined in the chorus. With sleepy eyes and grins on faces, those boys finished the song without missing a word.

Volumes have been written about manners and the rules of etiquette. We have touched on the main points in this chapter. Keep these closing words in your heart and you will be the most gracious hostess in town:

> If manners make the man, manners are the woman herself; because with her they are the outward and visible token of her inward and spiritual grace, and flow instinctively from the instincts of her inner nature.
> —CHARLES KINGSLEY

JILL RIGBY, speaker, columnist, author of *Manners of the Heart*, and President of The Business of Manners, believes respect for others is the beginning of humble confidence. Through elementary school programs, parenting workshops, and *The Business of Manners* for corporate hearts, Jill is a nationally recognized authority on manners in the marketplace, the classroom, and at home. You can contact Jill at www.mannersoftheheart.org.

Just Another Ordinary Meal or a Memorable Occasion?

MARY HUNT

NOW THAT you've mastered the planning and creation of a meal and basic etiquette for all occasions, there is still another very important element of entertaining: the presentation of your work. Yes, that's right; next to the actual taste and quality of the food, nothing will affect the outcome of a meal more than where and how it is served. Serve up a plain casserole on nice dishes with a linen tablecloth and you can entertain a variety of guests—from an evening with the boss's family to a luncheon with your coworkers. I bet that even your family will react differently if you try it with them, rather than serving dinner family style with paper napkins and the television on. Add a sprig of parsley, require them to wash their hands and put on clean shirts, and you can transform mealtime in your own home. And what did it cost you? A little extra for the bunch of parsley, and a little elbow grease getting the dust off those nice dishes.

> The ultimate purpose for preparing food is the communion that will take place while breaking bread together. —P. B. WILSON

I know it's worth it in my home. The reaction I get from my husband, Harold, and my two boys when I present dinner with a little extra flair is well worth the tiny bit of effort. And do you know why? It's because it tells them that I value them, that I value our time together, that they're special. When a guest (coworker, family member, or friend) in your home feels a sense of belonging and value, you have accomplished more than just creating a good meal.

When planning a dinner party or get-together, most of us spend all of our energies, budget, and time on the actual menu. But don't forget the presentation. It costs little if anything, but adds everything. You're creating an atmosphere to match your menu and the personalities of your guests. If you're creatively challenged, visit a library or newsstand and start looking through magazines, or turn on one of the TV shows that focuses on food and entertaining.

The sky is the limit when it comes to presentation. You've already accomplished the major portion of the event—the food. Now it's time to finish the job.

The Atmosphere

Where you choose to serve your meal has a lot to do with the happiness of your guests. The room's size, ventilation, and proximity to the kitchen should all be considered. A wonderful gourmet meal creates a mood, and the atmosphere must match that mood. Short of buying a new house or having your furniture recovered, think outside the lines and consider moving your meal to another room. Perhaps an intimate dinner in front of the fireplace with the glow of the fire and candles providing both warmth and light would be a good alternative.

If you have one of those wonderfully large kitchens, create a farmhouse effect with everyone dining in the kitchen, the aroma of the food delighting the senses. A kitchen creates a sense of security; it is the heart and soul of

> If you're charged with planning a company off-site sales meeting, luncheon, or dinner party, consider the atmosphere of a local restaurant or hotel conference room. Good food is only a part of the dining experience. The right atmosphere can relax guests and generate good feeling, but the wrong atmosphere could be a disaster.
>
> Though you may be planning an office event, people want and need an escape from problems and everyday surroundings. The location chosen should project a feeling of friendliness and comfort. After working all day, most people would prefer to eat in a quiet, relaxed, intimate atmosphere. However, that may not be the best environment for a "working" lunch. Therefore, it is very important to be thoroughly familiar with the purpose of the event, as well as with the people who will be attending.

many households, and it's no surprise we congregate there. It can be creatively decorated with lots of candles, arrangements of wild flowers and greens, and some of your more unusual serving pieces. The great thing about entertaining in the kitchen is that your menu and the mood can be more casual. (You might want to clean off the front of the fridge first!)

The Room

When guests arrive, whether you birthed them or they are "official" dinner guests, they always walk into your home and look around the room. And if they are of the male persuasion, they are on the lookout for food. Now, keeping in mind that having food tells them you think they are special, you had better have some ready. First impressions say a lot, and don't be discouraged if the first thing they see isn't the beautiful flower arrangement you put together yourself or the creatively set table. After all, your goal is to put them at ease and make them feel welcome, right? A hands-down favorite at my house for creating that wonderful feeling is the aroma of baking bread. If you're not a bread maker, some marvelous frozen breads are available.

Be creative in the way you serve your appetizers. Serve chips and popcorn in big baskets, or how about in the brim of a sombrero or cowboy hat? A little different perhaps, but you will have left a creative memory for your guests. And don't forget to add some visuals to your appetizer table. Whether it's a simple arrangement of greenery, a grouping of some collectibles you have, or a splash of color using linens, each food area needs your attention because that's where your guests will congregate.

The Table

For a sit-down meal, the table is the focus. I have gone to dinner parties where twelve people sat glued to their chairs talking, laughing, and eating for three to four hours without moving other than to help the hostess clear the dishes. If your goal is to make entertaining a priority, a large table with comfortable chairs should be on your list of furnishings to acquire someday.

Because we're inclined to sit at the table for hours, it's all the more important that the table presentation be appealing, inviting, and comfortable. How many can sit comfortably around your table? Unless you've invited sardines to your dinner party, no one wants to be greased up and stuffed into his seat. Until Harold and I created "Big Table," we were limited to ten. That was it, and I knew it. Realize what your limit is and stick with it.

Now, depending on the theme of your party—casual or formal, holiday or everyday—your table presentation will be built around that idea. Many hostesses think they have to spend lots of money on flowers, linens, and other accessories. Wrong. One woman, Paulette Hegg, sums up table presentation the best: "I don't have an open-ended food budget, so I feel it's a gift from me to my family and guests to make the food and table look good even if the meal by some standards is not gourmet."

Homegrown flowers and herbs and different sizes and shapes of candles can create a very inviting table. I am convinced that ivy was God's decorating gift to the dinner party hostess. I am among the millions of Americans who have ivy growing in my yard, and I use it abundantly in my decorating. Whether it lines a tray of appetizers, snakes through the candles on the table, or serves as a place card (yes, that's right—write your guests' names with a metallic pen on big green leaves), it adds more than a standard bouquet of flowers ever could. And the best part is—it's free. If you don't have ivy, I encourage you to make friends with your neighbor who does.

The Plate

Finally, we come to the fruits of your labor. There is an old adage about food that is so true: you eat with your eyes first. A simple but deft finishing touch can turn a visually neutral dish into one that's smashing. Garnishes add eye appeal and don't have to be time-consuming or put a strain on your budget. There is a rule of thumb, however, and that is that any garnish should be edible and, when possible, an ingredient that complements the dish. Just buy a little or snip a little extra of that herb, vegetable, or fruit for your garnish.

Another way to make your plate visually appealing is by being a little creative in the way a dish is displayed on the plate. Use your pastry bag to create a special look for mashed potatoes. Use a citrus stripper to flute mushrooms by carving out strips at even intervals. Present soups or stews in bowls lined with lettuce or spinach. Make scalloped edges in citrus fruits. Experiment with flower radishes. You get the idea.

Consider serving your meal in courses instead of all at once. This lengthens your evening and really places the emphasis during the meal on the food. The only limit is your imagination. Whatever you choose to do, the most important thing is for you to be relaxed and enthusiastic and for your guests to crave a return invitation.

MARY HUNT is founder and publisher of *Cheapskate Monthly,* author of the nationally syndicated column, "Everyday Cheapskate," and a financial columnist for *First for Women* magazine. Her books have sold more than one million copies, and she speaks widely on personal finances. Mary has been a guest on such television shows as *Oprah, Good Morning America,* and *The O'Reilly Factor,* and has been featured in magazines like *Real Simple* and *Business Week.* Mary and her husband live in Orange County, California.

Nutritional Know-how

JEAN KRUEGER

Our Health

As godly businesswomen, we have a certain responsibility toward each other as we prepare to entertain. We must think of *health*—of our bodies, our minds, and our spirits. They are all connected. If one is lacking, everything else suffers. Here are some shocking statistics:

- Obesity has reached epidemic proportions in the United States. The Surgeon General reports 64 percent of Americans are either overweight or obese. In 1980, that statistic was only 48 percent.
- Obesity is now the leading cause of avoidable death. (Smoking used to be number one.)
- Adult weight gain greatly increases women's risk for developing breast and uterine cancer.

> "Dear friend, I pray that you may enjoy good health and that all may go well with you, even as your soul is getting along well." (3 John 2)

- Adult weight gain significantly increases men's risk for developing colon and prostate cancer.
- Obese people experience considerably more sickness and disease than their slimmer counterparts, and their health care costs are 44 percent greater.

Entertaining with a Healthy Balance

What does that word *balance* mean? How does it fit into the way the godly businesswoman entertains? The dictionary lists the following synonyms for *balance:* symmetry, evenness, proportion. We don't have to be on a "diet." We can "live it" if we use moderation and offer a menu with healthful balance and nutrition.

The foods that give us the most healthful balance to good nutrition fall into these categories:

Fruits and Vegetables

Everyone needs a mix of five or more cups of fruits and vegetables a day. Fresh or frozen is best. Canned or processed fruits and vegetables do not have the same vitamins and minerals and contain preservatives, sodium, extra calories, and chemicals that some studies have linked to cancer.

Grains

Serve breads and cereals that are rich in fiber, such as whole grains. White breads and white flour are not only robbed of their nutritional value, but they also turn into sugar and awaken our cravings.

"A false *balance* is an abomination to the LORD, but a just weight is his delight." (Prov. 11:1, KJV, emphasis added)

Protein

Protein should be considered a condiment and the fruits, veggies, and grains should be the main event. We only need three to six ounces of lean protein a day to build and replace muscle. More can actually leach calcium from our bones. For vegetarians, beans and tofu are excellent sources of protein.

Calcium and Milk Products

Need calcium for strong bones and teeth. Low-fat milk or soymilk, low-fat cottage cheese and low-fat yogurt are all good sources. If they seem boring, consider serving a fruit smoothie with your favorite fruits and all or any of the above.

Fat

We do need a small amount of fat to aid digestion; however, fat seems to come our way naturally without our seeking it. Some fats are better than others. Consider avocados, salmon, or a small amount of olive oil as sources of good fats.

Suggestions to Lighten Up Our Menus

Talking about nutrition in an entertainment book seems like we're taking away all the fun, doesn't it? But it doesn't have to be that way. We can't take care of everyone's recommended daily allowances for vitamins when they are only with us for one meal, and we don't want to *not* have a hamburger cookout for the Fourth of July because we are worried about serving red meat and potato chips. But there are ways we can plan healthier options.

- Serve as many *fresh* foods as possible.
- Choose *leaner cuts* of meat.
- Use *herbs and spices* to flavor foods rather than salt, oils, and butter.
- Fried means cooked in fat. Opt for food that is *baked, broiled, or grilled* instead.
- Limit use of bad fat treats such as chips, frozen pizza snacks, and high-fat microwave popcorn. You can use them on occasion or can find substitutes.

Keep in mind that poor choices often stem from mindless routines, rituals, patterns, or customs. Here are seven bad choices that spell **FAILURE**:

- *Food with fat—these foods include sausage; pork; ham; and greasy, battered, or fried foods. If we eat fat, we wear fat!*
- *Abundance of portions in butter and white (not wheat) breads—white flour wakes up cravings; butter and margarine clog our arteries.*
- *Insistence on decadent desserts—they provide no real nutrition. Find low-calorie substitutes.*
- *Loads of creamer, sugar, and coffee—they retain water. They slow weight loss.*
- *Unnecessary salt, sugar, and white flour—these are the "Three Whites." They contribute to bloating and high blood pressure.*
- *Rich fats: dressings, cheeses, gravies, and sauces—all of these lead to high cholesterol, high blood pressure, and artery-clogging fat.*
- *Extinguishing thirst with food instead of water—we often think we're hungry, but we're really thirsty. Serve plenty of water.*

Keeping balance and portion control in mind are crucial. Butter, one of the main ingredients in cooking, contains a lot of fat and calories. One cup of butter contains 2,200 calories and a tremendous amount of fat. However, a simple substitution of one cup of unsweetened applesauce reduces the calories to 100 and the fat to almost zero. If you have never used applesauce in baking cakes or cookies, this may seem absurd, but I urge you to try it. It adds an interesting flavor—and moisture.

Oil is another source of calories. Try substituting canola oil, cooking spray, or products such as I Can't Believe It's Not Butter®. Sprays are better than solid margarine because they stay in liquid form. Anything in a tub is hydrogenated and causes plaque buildup in our veins and arteries, contributing to high blood pressure.

The best way to prevent overuse of salt is to not use prepackaged foods. Buy products that are low in sodium, or cook all foods without salt and let the guests add the amount they want.

🐭 It's Not How Much You Eat, It's What You Eat!

FIBERS are FRIENDS and CALORIES are CULPRITS. Even if you're not on a diet, the simple addition of high fiber foods will help stabilize your weight. Most fruits, vegetables, and grains are fibrous foods, which force your body to burn its own fat. Because they hasten weight loss, it is possible to eat larger quantities of these foods. Fresh pineapple is a good example. Four ounces contain 76 calories. Yet your body uses 100 calories to digest it. That means 24 calories are burned from your own body fat.

When fibrous foods are eaten along with fattening foods, the fibers, which contain pectin, bond to higher-calorie foods. (Think of how pectin is used to solidify jelly or jam.) Remember the concept of "beef in a leaf." Wrap beef (a fatty food) in a lettuce leaf (which contains pectin). The pectin bonds to the fat, and leaves the body faster, without doing as much harm. So eat salad all the way through your meal, or try to eat an apple along with your dessert.

High fiber foods sweep up all the poisons in your body. Their soluble fibers enter your blood stream and clear away the plaque in your veins. If you could see a cross section of cholesterol buildup in your veins and intestines, you would be reminded of a spooky cave with stalactites hanging down and stalagmites poking up. Those kinds of formations are the plaque that causes heart disease, high blood pressure, and many other disorders, including cancer.

Special Guests: Dietary Considerations/Special Needs

Special guests, special diets, food allergies, and food aversions can be worked into planning an event. However, it is up to the guest to let you know of these needs in advance.

Diabetics

If you're entertaining a guest who is diabetic, he or she will likely have a diabetic meal plan from a doctor and will know what and how much to eat. It's comforting to know many of the guidelines for diabetics are the same for all of us. The guidelines are all about balance, portion, and general guidelines for healthy eating. A diabetic needs a diet low in fat, sugar, and sodium. Here are some guiding principles:

- Watch the fats you add. One teaspoon of regular margarine or butter can add 45 calories. Too much oil and cheese can contribute to high blood pressure.
- Remember that fresh fruit is the best dessert.
- Roasted, skinless white meat of poultry and boiled, baked, broiled, or grilled fish or seafood are lower in fat and calories than beef or pork. If you serve red meat, choose leaner cuts.
- Raw, steamed, grilled, stewed, or baked vegetables are lower in fat than vegetable casserole salads made with mayonnaise. Skip the gravy and sauces, or use them sparingly.
- Coffee, unsweetened tea and water are acceptable beverages to have on hand.
- Here are some fruits with three grams of fiber or more per serving: raw blueberries, pomegranates, raspberries, strawberries, dried fruit, apples, apricots, figs, and prunes.

Elderly People

Elderly people may have difficulty chewing, and certain vegetables like broccoli and cauliflower cause them painful gas. If you know in advance that most of your guests will be elderly, it is best to serve soft foods and precooked mild veggies.

Kids

With children's parties, here are some ways to avoid too much sugar:

- Let the kids make their own fresh vegetable kabobs.
- Have plenty of finger foods in the form of vegetables and fruits, such as cherry tomatoes, grapes, and small carrots.

- Reduce the amount of sugar you add to recipes.
- Give gum as a prize/treat instead of candy.
- Serve water or milk or fruit smoothies instead of soda or sweet juice.

If we could change the *seven bad choices* listed earlier to the *seven good choices* that spell **SUCCESS** listed below, we will get away from mindless routines, rituals, patterns, or customs.

- **S**ubstitute spices for salt.
- **U**nderstand forbidden foods* undo progress.
- **C**ut cheeses, fats, sauces, dressings, and gravies.
- **C**hoose to discard coffee, creamer, and sugar.
- **E**xercise and extinguish hunger by enjoying water.
- **S**kip that petit four.
- **S**lip in more veggies and fruit.

JEAN KRUEGER is a health expert, speaker, and author of *Why the Weight? Dare To Be Great!,* a spiritual approach to weight loss. Once seriously overweight, Jean dropped sixty pounds, and her medical problems vanished. Now her passion is to help others do it too!

---

*Remember the forbidden foods are pork; ham; sausage; and greasy, fried, and battered foods.

Creating a Home of Excellence

RUTH HUSSEY HESS

I F SOMEONE rang your doorbell today and offered you an unlimited expense account for a complete home makeover, wouldn't you be excited? I know I would shriek for joy and open the door wide. Yes, having unlimited resources with which to decorate would be a dream come true for most of us. We long for that perfect space to share with others but, for many of us, our space just never seems to come together the way we would like. As a result, we hesitate to open our home to others, or we limit our hospitality to a circle of close friends.

Having a truly perfect home for entertaining is not beyond the scope of your imagination. Through many years of exercising my skill in hospitality, I have come to understand three elements essential to having the kind of home that beckons guests. Once I uncovered those key pieces to the puzzle, I learned to love my home. That is when God began to use our home as more than a place to eat, sleep, and watch television.

ᓚ Proper Focus

It has been surprising for me to learn that many women feel more adequate in the workplace than they do entertaining in their own homes. Women often tell me, "I can't entertain until we get new carpet, or hang new drapes, or buy new furniture, or paint the living room." Our society has built a picture of the perfect home with everything in its place, beautifully appointed with every creature comfort, and we feel our imperfect homes do not measure up. We hide behind our "if onlys" and miss out on the joy that comes with opening our homes to others. Many of us have forgotten that entertaining is all about people and not about things. Our focus must be on people and how we can make them feel warmed and welcome in the space we call home.

Your house may not be the home of your dreams. In fact it may be quite ordinary, but that's what excellence at home is all about. It simply means taking what is ordinary and making something special out of it. Too often, we confuse excellence with perfection and we never accept what we have at this moment. We wait in the wings for something more and are blinded to the possibilities of what God has already provided for us.

God is not looking for perfect homes and perfect hostesses. He is looking for imperfect homes, run by imperfect women who are available to turn every threadbare inch of their lives over to Him. Then *He* can make our hearts *and* our homes into works of excellence for His glory. Part of that excellence will be revealed as we focus on people and welcome them into our homes instead of waiting for that complete makeover with an unlimited expense account.

People will not admire us any more for what we have, but they will come to love *Him* more for what they see in us. The direction of our focus, not the limits of our resources, makes our home an excellent place in which to entertain. He is a God of limitless resources and endless vision. As we learn to put people first and work on aligning our focus with His, Christ will provide all we need to do the work of hospitality.

Develop Creativity

Even before we owned our own home, I prayed for creativity. I knew it was important and I knew God cared about it, because His creativity literally shouts to us from nature. It also occurred to me that I had to take action as I prayed. That thinking led me to feed my creativity by completing simple projects for our home. Those baby steps fueled my desire to develop increased creativity, and our home began to take shape. Here are some ways to develop increased creativity:

1. *Observation:* Improve your creative thinking by becoming more alert to the visual details of a picture, a room, or a piece of artwork. Notice what color combinations and styles look good together. Don't be afraid to jot down things you see when you're out and about, so you don't forget what appealed to you at that moment. You will soon develop a new sense of awareness as you begin to view artistic expression with purpose.

2. *Reflection:* Reflect on creativity through what I call a "style file." Using a simple filing system, perhaps one folder for each room of your home, begin to clip magazine pictures of interiors you love. Write down observations of things you have seen that reinforce your emerging style. Circle items on the pages, or make notations to indicate what appealed to you and why you cut the page out. Your file will grow fat with ideas. As you look through each folder and reflect on the contents, you will find yourself adding your own creative twist to the ideas you have gleaned.

3. *Implementation:* Select one simple idea from your file and figure out how to achieve the look on your own. At first, you may need instruction and encouragement, so get with a creative friend or find a practical book at the library that gives step-by-step directions. As you begin this practice phase of your creative growth, your steps may be uncertain, but with each new attempt, your creativity will grow. Before long, fresh thinking and ideas will begin to flow as if from nowhere!

Another amazing thing happened. I began to understand that true creativity is being able to see things not as they are, but as they could be. That led me to finding new purposes for unused objects to fill needs in our home. Several years ago when we moved into our current home, we really needed an additional chair in our larger living room. The budget said, "No!" Since we were soon to have a dinner party, I longed for that extra seat and tried to think of creative ways to make it happen. Just as I was about to give up, a trip to the attic revealed a very old twin poster bed the previous owner had left behind. I was ecstatic.

As soon as John came home that afternoon, I told him there was a great chair in the attic. He quickly checked it out and was disappointed to find a lovely old bed, which we did not need at all. I said, "Honey, it *looks* like a bed, but when we get finished with it, we'll have not just a chair but a *love seat.*"

Since by this time we had been married long enough for him to recognize that look in my eye, he didn't express any doubt. My sweet husband scrambled up and brought that bed down. In just three short hours, while I cheered him on, John transformed that little bed into the cutest love seat you have ever seen. The next day, a coat of paint and a king-sized pillow with a deep flounce finished the job and we proudly placed it in our living room. I could hardly wait for our guests to arrive so I could share our adventure with them. We didn't need a bed. We needed a chair, and God provided even more than what we needed in a most unusual way. We simply had to be willing to see the potential for change.

As you prepare your home for memorable moments of hospitality, don't hesitate to ask God to increase your creative thinking. Ask Him to help you see things not as they are, but as they could be. Don't be afraid to stretch the ideas you see all around you to meet your home's specific needs. You will soon find yourself developing all sorts of creative masterpieces, and then you won't hesitate to throw open the doors of your home and lovingly share it with others.

🐾 Attitude Adjustment

First impressions are important. We know it's true of people we meet, but we forget the same thing applies to our homes. Just ask any real estate agent. The "curb appeal" of your home can attract interest from people who don't even want to buy a house. If you're like me, when we are driving and come to an especially pretty house, I urge my husband to slow down. I want to take a nice long look. It doesn't matter if the house is huge and expensive, or even in the best neighborhood. What makes a difference is the "picture" it makes on the lot.

Your attitude is like curb appeal. It will resonate through your home. Your guests will even know what your attitude is by the way you use your home and the things that are in it. The more loving the attitude that spills from the corners of our homes, the more people enjoy the moments they spend within its walls. Our attitude can be Satan's biggest weapon to keep us from being effective in hospitality.

Each of us knows the attitudes with which we struggle. Sometimes it is pride; for some it is anger or an unforgiving heart. But whatever name we give it, that attitude can spill out and fill the rooms of our home. Our "curb appeal" is diminished because of it. People are not interested in spending time in our company or our homes or in sharing all that God has given us. Spending time with the designer of hearts can change your attitude and bring about irresistible changes to your home.

If you truly want a home that bears the designer's name so you can entertain with joy, you can have it by incorporating these three essentials into your decorating scheme.

Make sure you're focusing on loving people and making them feel at home, not on the material things you wish you had but don't.

- Consciously work on developing a higher level of creativity so you can enhance the space you live in and feel more comfort and pride in sharing it with others.

- Confront the attitudes you know are wrong, and like a terrible piece of furniture, banish them from your life. Doing this will brighten every corner of your home and cause people to bask in its warmth.

RUTH HUSSEY HESS is currently an adjunct professor at Cedarville University as well as a seminar presenter, writer, and former public school teacher. She has developed a ministry focused on excellence at home, speaks extensively on creativity, joyful living, and shares original decorating tips and entertaining techniques for women on the go.

Section Two
SPECIAL OCCASIONS

8

CHAPTER

Celebrations

DORIS K. CHRISTOPHER

I FEEL THAT celebrations serve as markers in our progress through life. The times when we gather with friends and family are wonderful for both reflection and renewal. We could write our emotional and spiritual autobiographies using celebrations as milestones. For example, which Christmas was it that I started thinking more about the gifts that I would give than the gifts that I would receive? When did Thanksgiving become a day of thought and prayer as well as a feast and a day off from school or work? How old was I when I realized how much more Independence Day was than fireworks and picnics?

When I list the fixed celebrations in my family's life, it's an impressive number: the great religious festivals, of course, and national events such as Veterans Day. Add in the traditional events like birthdays, anniversaries, baby showers, and baptisms, and I find my calendar filled with celebrations in each and every month. And yet, one thought keeps coming back to me: "I hope I didn't omit any opportunities to celebrate."

When you stop and think about it, most families have a great deal to celebrate nearly each and every day. You will find the opportunities there if you just take a moment and look for them: a good day (or week) at work, a new job or promotion, meeting a new friend, your child's high score on a test, a first tooth, winning sports teams, and so on. Celebrations are a wonderful time to bring family and friends together for everyday and special occasions. And, these are good times to begin a few new traditions. There are thousands of these seemingly "little" occasions that should be celebrated and honored. What a shame if we let them go by unnoticed. It is the little things that truly can make the difference in a friend or family member's life.

When we celebrate an event in someone else's life, we show that person much more than the fact that we remember his birthday. We're showing him that an event that has importance in his life has importance in ours as well. We can touch his life as much as he has touched ours. It's our way of reaching out and showing we care. Each time we honor our children's accomplishments, we help set the stage for them to flourish as successful adults. Perhaps that's why some of the sweetest celebrations of all are the ones that recognize our kids' achievements.

When Sammy Werner's T-ball team won its championship, his mother, Claire, used simple food coloring to turn her family supper into a tribute. The Werners ate orange mashed potatoes washed down with blue milk, in honor of Sammy's team colors. "Food coloring is fun, inexpensive, and easy," says Claire. "And it adds interest to foods kids won't otherwise eat. It amazed me how fast that blue milk disappeared!" These days, Sammy and his sister Ellie never know what rainbow shades they might find on their plates. Claire added purple coloring to the white cake mix for Ellie's Barney birthday cake. And green pancakes have become a weekend staple at the Werners' house.

As the Werners' story shows, kids love the little things that turn ordinary into extraordinary. There are as many of these opportunities to make the day special as there are families, and they needn't be costly or elaborate. The happy truth is that it takes surprisingly little to elevate a simple family meal into a spectacular one. Brightly colored milk in a special glass. Ice cream sundaes for dessert. Handcrafted place cards made by the kids. Celebratory traditions can be as easy as swapping seats, thereby giving the straight-A student or "most valuable player" the spot of honor at the head of the table. Families with round tables can accomplish much the same thing by serving their MVP first.

People remember the unexpected, or certainly the unscheduled, celebration. They remember the proud look in their parents' faces at their piano recitals. They remember the handshakes and slaps on the back that followed that hole in one. They remember coming to work and finding a sign saying, "Congratulations!"

One of the best examples I know of reaching out was a party my mother-in-law, Maxine Christopher, arranged for a neighbor. This man had no siblings or close relations and had lived with his mother most of his adult life. He married just a few years before his mother's death; then, only a few years later, his wife also died. My mother-in-law arranged a surprise party for his seventy-fifth birthday, inviting all the neighbors. This party meant everything to him. With tears in his eyes, he told the guests that it was the most special birthday of his long life, because everyone dear to him was gone. He hadn't realized that anyone else knew or cared about his birthday.

On that occasion, and on many others, my mother-in-law reached out. She actively looked for a moment to celebrate, for an opportunity to show someone he mattered. I try to bring some of the wonderful spirit she has modeled into my own life, and I feel blessed to have her as an example.

At The Pampered Chef, one of our most valued traditions is called Celebration. One day every month, all the coworkers gather for a party. We have balloons and music, and everyone wears casual clothing with the company logo. An officer of the company makes announcements, products are demonstrated, and then we reach out to each other's lives. Every coworker who has a birthday or whose anniversary of employment with the company falls in that month is given a gift. Coworkers applaud continuously as the names are read. Twice a year, everyone knows that the company and his or her coworkers will honor him or her.

When this tradition started, The Pampered Chef was a small company. In those days, all of us sat around one table. Today, with almost one thousand coworkers, we hold four parties on the same day—one for each of our two shifts in each of our two locations. Occasionally, some suggest that we shorten Celebration or even eliminate it. But I believe that Celebration is one of the occasions that makes The Pampered Chef what it is today. I love to see the faces of the coworkers light up with pride when their name is called. I know that we have reached out to that person and said, "We know this is an important day in your life, and it's important to us, too." It is just one way we can show our pride in our coworkers as we reward and recognize their work.

Nothing beats a birthday celebration, with the possible exception of two celebrations. In the case of the Graff family, it's more like a celebration and a half. "Chris and I started celebrating our children's 'half-birthdays' when they were little," Nancy Graff says, "but the ritual proved so popular, we've kept right on doing it, even though my son Garrett is now a junior in high school and my daughter Lindsay is in seventh grade."

Her kids' half-birthdays, celebrated six months to the day after their actual birthdays, consist of special dinners of their choosing, and they differ from their true birthdays in several important ways.

Instead of a whole cake, Nancy serves half a cake, with half the usual number of candles on top. There's just one present, costing no more than twenty dollars. And the guest list is limited to Garrett, Lindsay, Nancy, and Chris. "Real birthdays involve other people, but on half-birthdays, the focus is just on the family," explains Nancy. "And half-birthdays aren't really about presents. They're more about being almost ready to drive, or being almost a teenager."

Those of us who have celebrated dozens of birthdays tend to forget how significant turning a year older can be to a child. Each birthday brings some exciting new privilege, from starting school to paying the adult price at the movies, and all deserve recognition at family celebrations. Indeed, some birthdays deserve special treatment, since they imply a rite of passage that's particularly noteworthy. For my daughter Kelley's Sweet Sixteen, we had a cake that resembled a driver's license. When Alison Caplain turned thirteen, her mother Marcy planned a special women-only celebration, followed by a hairstyling session and a department store makeover.

Regardless of age or motif, younger kids' birthdays can be easily put together by one or two adults using standard components: other kids, a fun activity, ice cream and cake, along with presents, paper plates, and plenty of napkins. But as we get older, the formula changes as our focus shifts from presents to people. And for the people who love us, that can lead to a different sort of celebration—the kind that comes from the heart, as opposed to the shopping mall.

Lynn Jonas used to buy her grandmother Sarah jewelry or clothes for her birthday. But now she buys groceries instead. The special birthday dinners she cooks for her grandmother every June are made all the more meaningful by the distance Lynn travels to make them—nearly two hundred miles each way, from her home in southern Connecticut to her grandmother's in central New Hampshire. The food is secondary to the ritual, which is all about spending time together. And for Lynn, there's no better place to celebrate than in her grandmother's old-fashioned kitchen. "Every item on the table brings back memories: the salt and pepper shakers, the sugar bowl, the coffee creamer. In fact, my grandmother still keeps them all on the same orange paint-by-numbers tray I made for her when I was seven!"

In my experience, that isn't unusual, but it's remarkable. Heirlooms are important to families, and they often play a significant role in celebrations. A great-aunt's hand-embroidered tablecloth or the Waterford candlesticks that passed through Ellis Island in Grandmother's steamer trunk speak to us of continuity and stability, heritage and love. But even the simplest objects—like handmade paper place cards—can take on mythic proportions when they embody a sentiment that comes from the heart.

I know of one family who covers their table with an ordinary white sheet that turns into a giant greeting card after their guests have signed it. Couples can adapt this tradition for anniversary celebrations by writing each other notes on the tablecloth year after year, thereby turning a sheet into a gigantic love letter, a record of their life together.

There is no better lesson to impart to our family and friends than the simple acts that give meaning to life. This is where the purest forms of celebrations arise. It's up to each of us to decide how to teach this, but a table blessing is a good place to start. Expressing our gratitude for all that we have is a wonderful habit to get into, because the better we get at seeing the good things, the more we are able to see. And the better we get at transforming our tables into all that we want them to be.

In the process, we find something magical happens. Life's noises and daily distractions fade into the background. Over roast beef or spaghetti, we listen and learn, cope and compromise, remedy and resolve. And we celebrate, with blue milk and orange mashed potatoes, handmade place cards and cakes cut in half. We giggle and argue and pass the potatoes. We dance to life's music, and we come away humming the tune. By transforming our tables, we transform our lives.

It is with that melody in my heart that I wish you to fill your calendars with a lifetime of special celebrations—happy birthdays and half-birthdays, work and winning T-ball championships. I hope this will be just the beginning, and that you and your loved ones will go on to create your own special rituals and celebrations, your own traditions and wonderful times.

ALL-AMERICAN CELEBRATION CAKE

For a star-spangled finale, serve this easy berry-topped cake complete with sparkling candles.

1	package (16 ounces) angel food cake mix	$^{1}/_{2}$	pint fresh raspberries (about 1 cup)
1	lemon	1	container (8 ounces) frozen whipped topping, thawed
$^{1}/_{2}$	cup powdered sugar		
3	cups strawberries, sliced (12 ounces)		Fresh mint leaves (optional)
$^{1}/_{2}$	pint fresh blueberries (about 1 cup)		

1. Preheat oven to 350 degrees. Prepare cake mix according to package directions. Pour batter into ungreased **Stoneware Rectangular**

Baker (9 × 13 in.), spreading evenly. Bake on center rack in oven 35–40 minutes or until top is golden brown and the cracks feel dry and not sticky. (Cake should be firm to the touch; do not under bake.) Carefully turn baker upside down onto cooling rack; cool completely. (Do not remove cake from baker.)

2. Zest whole lemon. Juice lemon to measure 2 tablespoons juice. Whisk lemon juice, zest, and powdered sugar in large bowl until smooth.

3. Add strawberries, blueberries, and raspberries to sugar mixture; mix gently to coat fruit.

4. Using large fork, poke holes in cake about one and one-half inches deep and one-half inch apart. Spoon fruit mixture over cake to within one-half inch of edges. Refrigerate at least 2 hours to allow juices to soak into cake.

5. Just before serving, pipe whipped topping evenly around edge of cake. To serve, cut into squares. Garnish each serving with additional whipped topping and mint leaves, if desired.

Yield: 15 servings

Pictured left to right: Julie Christopher, Doris Christopher, Jay Christopher, and Kelly Christopher

(Low Fat) Nutrients per serving: Calories 190, Total Fat 3 g, Saturated Fat 3 g, Cholesterol 0 mg, Carbohydrate 37 g, Protein 3 g, Sodium 220 mg, Fiber 1 g

Diabetic exchanges per serving: 1 starch, 1½ fruit, ½ fat (2½ carb)

Cook's Tips: This cake can be prepared up to 6 hours in advance.

Use a serrated bread knife to easily cut through the tender angel food cake.

©The Pampered Chef, Ltd., 2001

DORIS K. CHRISTOPHER is the founder and chairman of The Pampered Chef, the premier direct seller of high-quality kitchen tools. Doris and her husband, Jay, reside in the Chicago suburbs near their daughters, Julie and Kelley.

The material used within this chapter was adapted from the book COME TO THE TABLE: A Celebration of Family Life *by Doris K. Christopher. Copyright © 1999 by Doris K. Christopher. Reprinted by permission of Warner Books, Inc, New York, NY. All rights reserved. For more information visit* www.pamperedchef.com.

Breakfasts and Brunches

Linda Overton

HAVE YOU discovered the joy and excitement of entertaining with breakfast and brunches? Preparing a morning meal for your friends, family, or coworkers can be a simple yet rewarding experience.

This popular form of casual entertaining is generally a welcome change from the standard business luncheon or dinner party, and can be enjoyed in the comfort of your home or planned for the office or an off-site location.

The key is simplicity. Whether the event is on the spur of the moment or planned months in advance, keeping it simple will allow an atmosphere that will be relaxing and enjoyable to everyone.

Sunday family breakfasts were a celebration when I was a child. Before heading off to church, Dad would create the masterpiece and the rest of us would gobble it up as if it were the first time in days that we had eaten. We delighted in homemade biscuits and gravy with eggs, bacon, sausage, and hash browns. We treasured those moments by sitting together at the seldom-used kitchen table and breaking bread. We took the time to learn about each other's dreams, hope, desires, and heartaches.

Each year on January 1, almost forty years later, that same breakfast is served. Our family once again comes together at my parents' home to begin

Pick one day a week or a month to have a special gathering for breakfast or brunch for your family. It will change your life forever. Our family has opted for a special Saturday early to rise sunshine breakfast. The morning begins at 7:30 as my five-year-old son and I toss flour around the kitchen and whip up pancakes from scratch. The purpose is to make fond memories out of simple meals. Each week the recipe changes a little adding banana and pecans, chocolate chips or peanut butter. We make homemade syrups from chocolate, maple, and blueberry. You can even purchase wild-colored syrups now at the grocery. Whipped cream and fresh fruit make any pancake a delight—and don't forget the sprinkles on the top.

the New Year together. For us, this breakfast is a joyful tradition. A morning gathering can become the same for you and yours.

Planning

As with any occasion, start your brunch or breakfast with a plan. Your preparedness will determine the ease of execution of both the meal and event. It doesn't matter whether the event will be at your home or office or in a restaurant.

Home Preparation

If guests will be coming to your home, provide very comfortable and warm surroundings. I would strongly advise that you do the deep cleaning of your home several days before. Retouch the bathrooms and the eating area again the evening before the big day. If you can, have professionals clean all or part of your home. That will leave you more time for the breakfast details—and serve as a little treat for you!

Decorating

Decorate the night before your guests arrive. Decorations can be simple or elaborate. The little things do make a difference, but do not have to take up the majority of your time. You will spend less time actually doing the chore if you plan it and walk it through on paper and in your head.

Consider the room's layout. Where will the food be placed? What about the decorations? How will people flow into and out of the room? Will you serve family style, as a buffet, or with set plates? Consider all your options.

If you don't have a knack for decorating, don't be afraid to ask a friend to help. I have a friend who is a great cook—but if you asked her to decorate the table, she would dump in the center of the table a faded orange-and-yellow plastic flower arrangement she's had for thirty years. We have been friends for twenty years, and I'm happy to trade out about an hour of my time to help prepare for special events. Her payment to me is a meal to go for my family.

Decorations can be as simple as fresh flowers or a collection of salt and pepper shakers, teacups, candles, flat marbles, or stones. At a breakfast for my son's friends, we took all his colorful wood building blocks and made little monuments and buildings all through the serving line as well as on the table. The serving line was a coffee table that was placed at just the right height for youngsters. Their eating table was kid-size picnic benches. It was nothing fancy and rather simple. It also let me include my child in the fun.

Food Preparation

Prepare as much as possible the night or day before. Casseroles ready to cook and all cooked meats can be prepared and kept in the refrigerator.

Set your serving line or table as if the food were already prepared and in the serving dishes. Determine what dish or platter you want to use for each food that will be on your line. Set out the serving dishes in order. Place a little note card in each empty dish reminding you what you're going to place in it.

We prefer baking turkey bacon rather than frying or microwaving. If you place it on cookie sheets and bake it at 350 for twenty-five to thirty minutes, you will have perfect bacon. Then let it cool, place it in a storage bag in the refrigerator until it's time to reheat and serve the bacon.

Pick up your bakery-ordered breads and pastries as early in the day as possible. If you're going to another location for the event, plan to pick up the baked goods along the way. When ordering bagels, request that they be cut with a bread slicer. The presentation will be nicer and will give guests an opportunity to try more than one kind.

Guest Lists/Invitations

Is your breakfast or brunch for coworkers, family, friends, or post-prom breakfast party for your graduating high school senior?

The next step is to determine how many people the location can accommodate. For example, it is not advisable to have twenty people sitting in a space meant for eight. When you know how big a crowd you want or care to handle, then make up your list for invitations.

Invitations should be sent to a formal or casual event. The tone of the invitation will set the mood for the event. If the breakfast is casual, the invitation should be. If the invitation is on fine linen paper and resembles a wedding invitation, your guests will expect something more formal.

Location

The kitchen or dining room in your home does not have to be the location for a spectacular event. Depending on the number of guests and the tone of your brunch or breakfast, you can be creative in where you will have the party. If it is a group of ladies, why not a tearoom, a museum, aquarium, a front porch, a park, or flower garden? It always helps to have a kitchen close by but with planning, you can hold your event almost anywhere. Hot food pack carriers are perfect for just these occasions. They can keep your food hot or cold up to three hours.

If the breakfast will be at your work site, possible locations can include conference rooms, executive lounges, lobbies (before opening to public) and company kitchens. Ask your landlord if any other spaces are available for events. An atrium or library might be the perfect place for your group.

If you're planning your breakfast for a restaurant, visit the establishment before you make a commitment. Will it seat your group comfortably? Is the environment or surrounding what you want for this event? Visit the restaurant at the same time of morning that you plan to have your brunch or breakfast to check out the acoustics. Will you be able to carry on a conversation without shouting? If not, does the restaurant have private rooms large enough to seat your group?

Arrange to stop by the day before to review the menu and other details with the manager. You generally will have had to decide long before this time whether the meal will be served sit-down or buffet style, and what items will be served in either case. Meet with your servers as well to go over your expectations.

If you're hosting a larger group, it may be wise to preselect the menu and let your guests review the items in advance. Sometimes the restaurant will accommodate you in that area, as well as make up special menus if necessary. This will limit special orders and delays on the day of the event.

If you're serving breakfast to a group of six-year-olds, building a tent in the living room is an option. Put plastic on the floor and drape sheets over kitchen chairs. Throw in some party lights and this will make for a lasting memory for any child. If you're brave enough to undertake this adventure, serve the kids juices and milk in non-spill containers and offer dry cereal, doughnut holes, and cut up fruit such as pineapples, apples, and bananas. I would not recommend serving anything red or dark colored unless you want new carpet.

Menu Selection

What you serve depends in large part on whom you're serving. If you're preparing for a household of young men, consider a hearty brunch of scrambled eggs, breakfast casserole, bacon, ham, turkey bacon, summer sausages, pork sausages, hash browns, grits, biscuits, and gravy. You may also want to try a breakfast pizza made with crescent rolls. For a more elegant affair, consider éclairs, breakfast pastries, crepes, mini-quiches, fresh fruit, and citrus punches. If it's a corporate brunch, ask your team members about their favorite breakfast foods and special dietary needs.

BREAKFAST PIZZA

1   large can of uncooked crescent rolls; unroll and form onto a round pizza pan

Pour on top of that

4   eggs uncooked but scrambled
1½   cups of cooked pork sausage
1½   cups of grated/shredded pizza cheese or cheddar

Bake at 350 degrees for about 15 minutes until eggs are cooked, bread is slightly brown, and cheese has melted.

PARTY PIZZA SQUARES

2   packages of cocktail Rye bread (baby bread)
1   8 oz. package of Kraft Velveeta® Cheese shredded

1   pound of cooked pork sausage, turkey sausage, turkey or crumbled bacon

Take your cocktail bread and place each little slice side by side on a cookie sheet. Take the cooked meat and distribute to your liking over each piece of bread. Sprinkle shredded Velveeta over the meat and bake at 350 until cheese has melted.

WAFFLE RECIPE

3	cups flour	4	beaten egg whites
3	teaspoons baking powder	4	beaten egg yolks
1	teaspoon salt	2	cups milk
2	tablespoons sugar	4	tablespoons oil

In a bowl, combine dry ingredients. Stir in egg yolks. Add milk and oil, stirring until batter is lumpy. Fold in egg whites. Bake in a hot waffle iron. Remove carefully and brush with butter. Top with powdered sugar, fresh fruit, and your favorite syrup.

The Finishing Touches

It is not necessary to theme every meal, but a special occasion or even the simple addition of a touch of color can help establish the ambiance and the atmosphere you desire.

These touches can be as simple as adding linens to the table or putting a stable box or crate on the table and covering it with fabric. Scrunch the material around the base of the box to give it a gathered effect. Place your serving tray on top of the box and add some greenery, lighting, or décor. It is simple but beautiful with little effort.

White Christmas twinkle lights are great for adding pizzazz to any event. You also can purchase rope lighting in white and other colors to add a WOW effect. It looks like you spent days creating something that took less than five minutes.

You can never use too many doilies. Place some of the white paper variety under your food on serving trays to provide an elegant effect. Use the large ones as the place settings for the table and use the small ones for the glasses. You can make a glazed doughnut look like a gem placed on a white doily with the silver platter hidden underneath.

Don't forget to play some background music. It will set the tone and even calm your soul before the event begins.

You want a warm aroma, but not one of burnt toast. I like to heat some apple juice with a few cinnamon sticks and cloves thrown in. It gives you that warm fuzzy feeling of a chilly winter night sitting by the fireplace. Flavored coffees brewing are wonderful aromatherapy too.

Enjoy your breakfast and brunch, and don't forget to invite me.

LINDA OVERTON has more than twenty years' experience as an event planner for businesses, ministries, and individuals. Some of her more prestigious events include entertaining at the Jimmy Carter Presidential Library, private yacht parties at sea, and large corporate galas. Linda is also a business professional in the publishing industry with her most important role being that of wife and mother to her two favorite men—husband Keith and son Mitchell.

Luncheons

Sherry Taylor Cummins

MARTHA, THE FAMOUSLY hospitable sister of Mary and Lazarus, meets our Savior in the street and invites him to her home for a meal. "As Jesus and his disciples were on their way, he came to a village where a woman named Martha opened her home to him" (Luke 10:38). Martha had a serving heart. Modeling our own hearts after Martha's, a luncheon is the perfect venue for serving and giving to others at home, socially, or at work.

Luncheons are occasions for "soul" food—feeding your guests' physical appetites delightful cuisine and their spiritual appetites encouragement and enthusiasm. Your desired outcome is to create a respite in the middle of the day, an oasis of peace that is both calming and rejuvenating.

Sharing the Father

The purpose of your luncheon helps to determine how to proceed. A business meeting with a half hour scheduled to grab a casual bite requires a different approach than an elegant bridal luncheon. Regardless of the purpose, luncheons share a common focus, "And let us consider how we may spur one another on toward love and good deeds" (Heb. 10:24). Even on occasions where guests do not share your love of God, you, as the hostess, have a golden opportunity to share His love through special attention to your guests and the luncheon details.

You may find yourself overwhelmed like Martha as you plan. But Martha was distracted by all the preparations that had to be made. She came to him and asked, "Lord, don't you care that my sister has left me to do the work by myself? Tell her to help me!" "Martha, Martha," the Lord answered, "You are worried and upset about many things, but only one thing is needed. Mary has chosen what is better, and it will not be taken away from her" (Luke 10:40–42). As you move toward your goal of a successful luncheon, focus on the enjoyment and pleasure of your guests. This chapter will assist you in avoiding last-minute frustrations by outlining the basics of a luncheon as well as helpful, fun tips to make your planning smooth, easy, and exciting. Your luncheon will be one that you and your guests will look forward to, enjoy, and discuss for weeks after.

Begin with a Prayer

Begin with a prayer. "Ask, and it will be given you; seek, and you will find; knock, and it will be opened to you" (Matt. 7:7). When you ask the Master to work with you, you will benefit from the composure and confidence needed to plan a phenomenal event!

Put It in Writing

Write plans in a notebook. For a luncheon, you say? Indeed. Record details for easy reference. Should an unforeseen circumstance take you away, you can hand off the plan with assurance to a backup person.

The Details: Date, Time, Venue, and Theme

Be aware of any other events that may be affected by or that may affect your luncheon. Post the selected date on important calendars such as that of the venue, caterer, and club officers.

Begin the luncheon between 11 A.M. and 12:30 P.M. If it starts too early, people will not be hungry. Too much later in the afternoon, and it may interfere with dinner appetites.

Choose the location that provides the best setting for your luncheon. Book it early! If you have several choices for venue, deciding the theme in advance will assist you in making the perfect choice.

Decide on a theme based upon the event's purpose. The theme will guide you to colors and decorations. For one working lunch, I served pizza on red and white tablecloths. A large red rose with a long white ribbon and candles graced the table. Frank Sinatra crooned in the background. Even a quick break in the corporate day can benefit from decorations and will distract the working mind for a little while. Theme is the jump start to creativity.

Get the Word Out

You have a fabulous luncheon in the works and it is time to get the word out. Your invitation may be an e-mail sent to all attendees of a business meeting informing them that lunch will be provided. You may casually phone family members to invite them to the holiday luncheon you're planning in your home, or mail a formal written invitation for a garden party at a restaurant. Include the date, time, and venue address. Also include an RSVP date, contact name, and phone number so you know how many guests for which to plan.

About Caterers

Word of mouth is the best way to find a good caterer. If you find a caterer in the telephone book, ask for references. I used local and reputable caterers for three years before I tried a newly recommended caterer. I have used the new caterer almost exclusively since then. He has a flexible menu from which I can select pizza for casual meals, barbecue for outdoor fun, salads for lighter tastes, and chicken marsala for formal luncheons. The caterer is willing to work with me, providing many options and offering to create requests. He delivers, sets up, picks up, and invoices. He arrives on time, the food is good,

LUNCHEON THEMES

Theme	Colors	Decorations
Garden Party	Pinks, Reds, Greens	Flowers, Teapots
Country	Red/Green Plaid, Any Color Gingham	Hurricane Lamps
Winter Wonderland	Ice Blue, Navy Blue, White, Silver	Snowflakes, Stars
Valentines	Pink, Red, White, Purple	Hearts, Flowers
Celestial	Blue/Silver or Black/Gold	Stars, Moons, Candles
Mardi Gras	Purple, Gold, Green	Masks, Beads
Fall	Orange, Gold, Green, Purple	Leaves, Scarecrow
Spring	Pastels	Umbrellas, Ducks
Summer	Red, White, Blue	Baseball, Sunglasses

the price is oh so right, and he takes pride in his work and in our relationship. What a find!

When using a caterer, request a quote and a contract in writing to prevent misunderstandings. For very large or important events, request a "tasting." A tasting provides an opportunity to sample the proposed menu. Tastings have saved the day for me more than once and resulted in changes from my original menu plans.

The Menu—Art of the Heart

Ah, the menu. Selecting the menu is like painting a picture. Color, texture, and design are so important. And, don't forget dessert. Chocolate—delicious, dark, and decadent—is a mouthwatering must for a successful luncheon (it has never failed me). There are additional factors—time, other meals in the day, and diversity—that figure into selecting the foods that will adorn each plate and help to create this art of the heart.

Is this a quick luncheon break for a conference or a leisurely lunch for a club membership who can linger all afternoon? More time means more options.

What will be happening for the dinner hour? If this is a group of people who will be sharing a heavy dinner together, you will want to serve lighter food. If your attendees will be traveling home and spending time in an airport, provide a more substantial lunch.

How diverse are your guests? You won't want to serve pork out of respect for your Jewish guests, and you will absolutely want to serve tea to your Japanese guests. To accommodate most tastes, you might consider a buffet rather than a plated luncheon, or you might choose to provide two main courses.

Luncheon Logistics

Conversation among your guests will be encouraged by round tables. Eight is the perfect number for best conversation. Mingle newcomers and people who know each other well in your seating plan.

Arrange all AV equipment you're using, and test it in advance. If you have a speaker, ask what requirements that person may have, such as a lectern, a microphone, or projection equipment.

Name tags are necessary if everyone is not acquainted. Print the name tags in advance and display them on a table at the entrance to the dining area. Place cards are not always necessary, but they certainly add a special touch to

---

FOUNTAINS AND ICE SCULPTURES

Fountains and ice sculptures add atmosphere. You can make an ice sculpture yourself if you have a large enough freezer. Food service companies have molds for order. Ask for directions with the mold. Fountains are available for rental and may be used as decorations with colored water or may be filled with punch as a unique way to serve.

a formal event. If the seating is assigned, place cards are required. Print on the card the name of the guest and the number of the table where the guest will be seated. Put a numbered sign on each table, large enough so that guests may see the number easily.

Atmosphere, Atmosphere, Atmosphere!

Luncheon planning changed for me when I decided to take extra care with one particular meeting at our corporate headquarters. The directors and managers had traveled from all over the country. They were on their second day of meetings, tired and ready to go home. Usually, I serve buffet style, which is the custom in the office since serving lunch is just one of my many responsibilities.

HELPFUL HINTS

- Keep decorations in clear plastic stackable drawers for easy viewing. Store and label by color or season for easy access.
- Enlist the aid of a helper—someone to greet guests, remember last-minute details, help decorate, etc.
- Display food at different levels by using baskets underneath tablecloths.
- Stack square napkins in the palm of your hand. Turn a full soda can on its side and move it in a circle on top of your stack to fan the napkins. Continue this action until the fan is as loose as you like.
- Use a color wheel for stunning color combination ideas such as blue and orange. They are opposites on the color wheel and therefore pleasing together!
- Holiday icicle lights provide a beautiful effect when clipped under a white table skirt. A clip can hold one tablecloth and two strings of lights. Use two colors together such as white and blue for winter and white and pink for sweetheart luncheons.

This time, I ordered salad as the entrée. I plated each salad on paper plates with an autumn theme. Each roll was plated and garnished with two pats of butter. The plastic cups were filled with orange and red napkins, shaped into flowers. Each guest had a place card. The plasticware was placed as if it came from Grandma's silver chest. Down the center of the oblong table were red and orange paper leaves and fall-scented candles. I lit the candles and lowered the lights slightly. My investment was just a few more minutes of time and no additional cost or tools than if I had set up a buffet. But the dividends were priceless. I wish you could have seen the faces of the directors and managers as they entered the room. The result? An afternoon of business that was less stressful and more productive. All because of atmosphere!

Little details are key to a great atmosphere. My favorite tools are simple. I utilize tablecloths and napkins, linen or paper, to fold, fan, scrunch, and cover levels on top of a base tablecloth. Start with a patterned napkin and work around the colors in that napkin. Use a large centerpiece and build around it. Where do I get my tools? White sales, garage sales, secondhand stores, and donations— anywhere I can acquire those valuable tools that make my luncheons more interesting and inviting.

If using a hall or renting a room, check with the proprietor on what you may use such as confetti, streamers, candles, and so on and what will be provided free of charge. Fountains, ice sculptures, colored linens, and lighted trees are among the decorations owners have provided to me gratis.

The most important rule in creating atmosphere is to step out. Do not be afraid. Brainstorm. Stretch your imagination. If your idea doesn't work, no harm is done. Keep trying until you're comfortable with this gift of creativity.

Tools of the Trade

Staples you can't live without:

- Candles (tapers, votives, and tea lights work best and are quite affordable)
- Baskets in all shapes and sizes (One of my favorite baskets is a gold wicker star that holds napkins or silverware upright.)

- Patterned and solid paper napkins
- Solid tablecloths in a variety of colors
- Silk flowers in pastels, autumn colors, deep jewel colors, and sparkly picks and green vines
- Ribbon in several widths and colors
- Containers in all shapes and sizes (I use three beautiful green hand-painted flower pots to hold knives, forks, and spoons.)
- Boxes of all shapes and sizes covered with wrapping paper
- Mini-Christmas tree lights in several colors
- Cloth napkins (if the budget allows)
- Large bead necklaces (like those used for Mardi Gras)

At Last

The big day is finally here. Arrive early to the location to double-check details against your written plan and so that you can place on the tables any last-minute items such as party favors, place cards, or programs. Greet your guests warmly. Shake hands firmly and with sincerity.

Start on time. Guests may have to return to work or may have other plans for the day. Follow your program as closely as possible. End with something that is thought-provoking as well as a memento of the special event. Thank each guest for attending as they leave.

Wrap-Up

The luncheon is over. Was it a success? Write down your thoughts in the planning notebook you started earlier—what worked, what didn't, what you would change, what you would add, and so forth.

A Prayer of Thanks

Congratulations! You did it. Now bask in the afterglow of hospitality done right, giving thanks to the One who made it so successful—your heavenly

Father. Say a prayer of thanks to God for bringing you this opportunity and for bringing momentary refuge to your guests. Keep your heart open, for I'm sure there is another opportunity to provide an oasis of peace just around the corner.

SHERRY TAYLOR CUMMINS is a freelance writer with contributions published in *Hearts at Home* magazine and faith-based anthologies. She works in Human Resources, Training, and Leadership Development in Ann Arbor, Michigan. Sherry has two grown children, a son-in-law, and two beautiful grandchildren. Sherry is currently working on her first novel.

Hospitalitea

PENELOPE CARLEVATO

A WONDERFUL WAY to share "hospitalitea" is having an afternoon tea. Most of the preparation can be done ahead of time, which gives you the chance to relax and share the time with your guests. An atmosphere of days gone by is created, and we succumb to an afternoon of luxury. Many of our friends love tea parties and are delighted to be invited. I have found it to be an encouraging way to share the love of Jesus.

An afternoon tea is usually scheduled from mid to late afternoon and is suitable for a variety of occasions. If you have been thinking of hosting an event or celebration, and would like something not so involved as a dinner party, an afternoon tea might be just what you want. I have given teas for birthday celebrations, wedding receptions, bridal and baby showers, christenings, and simply as intimate occasions to spend time with a few friends. Teas can be very formal affairs or as simple as a pot of tea and a package of store-bought cookies. I believe that God delights in our taking time for fellowship. In our "microwave" world, spending time sharing "hospitalitea" is an "opportunitea" to reach out in love to others. "Share with God's people who are in need. Practice hospitality" (Rom.12:13).

Everyone has the gift of hospitality. The way we express that gift is as unique as our personalities. We can be expressive with the things God has given us to use for His glory. We may not have a large home for entertaining or unlimited budgets. Most of us can't run out and buy a silver tea service, but we can be creative with what we have. Let me encourage you to ask others to your home, instead of meeting at the neighborhood coffee shop.

My mother was from England, so taking tea was a way of life for our family. Mother taught me to tea and had a wonderful gift of hospitality. I have tried to follow in her footsteps, and have converted many of my coffee-drinking friends. We all notice that something changes when the teacups come out and the tea is steeping. There is a calmness that isn't found in restaurants or coffee shops.

Mother had a delightful saying that has been a great help to me when I entertain: "Do what you can, where you are, with what you have!" Maybe you have a set of china that never gets used. Most china sets have cups and saucers and luncheon or dessert plates. You might even have a teapot that your aunt or grandmother gave you years ago. Take inventory. I am amazed what women tell me they find in their kitchen cabinets and china cabinets. Even if you don't have a set of china, use your everyday dishes and place a paper doily on the plate and a smaller one under the cup. You will be surprised how something so simple can change the tea table.

I have quite the collection of teacups and teapots. Most of them have been purchased at garage sales, thrift stores, or antique shops. Some were passed on to me when my Mother died, and others were gifts. Before I had enough teacups to go around, I would ask my friends to bring their own. We would tell how we acquired that particular cup and have a great time sharing stories. God has used these afternoon teas as a tool to reach women, to love them, and to develop relationships that have lasted many years. I have taught tea seminars and spoken to thousands of women about "hospitalitea." It has been such a joy to pass on my love of tea to others and see how God duplicates the desire to open homes for Him.

One young woman in California wanted to have teas to reach her neighbors, but had only a couple of teacups. I suggested going out early Saturday mornings and scouring garage sales. Several weeks later, she called and shared her exciting story. She had finally found a lovely bone china teacup from England. When she asked the lady having the sale if she had more, the lady took her inside and sold her six more cups and saucers and the shelf that held them—all for thirty dollars. That friend has been having her neighbors and friends to tea ever since. I know that God has used my tea "passion" and His love for others to encourage women to make a difference in their neighborhoods. My hope is that you will too.

Taking tea in the afternoon originated in the 1800s and was perfected during the reign of Queen Victoria. Many of the traditions or "rituals" celebrated during the tea ceremony are a direct result of her entertaining style. Tea can be served in the living room, dining room, or kitchen, on the porch or even on a picnic. I even take a tea party in a basket to friends who are sick.

There are three different types of tea parties. The traditional afternoon tea consists of three courses and is served mid-afternoon. Small, crustless tea sandwiches are the first course, then scones with jam and Devonshire cream, with the grande finale: tea cakes, tarts, and cookies. High teas are usually served after 5 P.M. and are not more elaborate, but the evening supper of the British working class. This is a heartier meal than the traditional afternoon tea, usually including some sort of meat dish. The third, a "cream" tea, is my favorite. It's easy to prepare and still rather elegant. Put on the kettle, bake a batch of scones, and serve them with jam and Devonshire cream. This is the perfect tea to take in the tea party basket. No matter which of the three teas you decide to serve, your guests will feel special. The clinking of china teacups, taking the time to relax, and celebrating the ritual of tea itself, makes it the perfect way to offer hospitality. Maybe that's one of the reasons teas are increasing in popularity.

I still remember the first afternoon tea I prepared with my friend Carol. We pooled our collection of teapots and teacups, practiced making light and

---

BRITISH HIGH TEA

Pot of hot tea
Scotch Eggs (hard boiled egg, shelled, with sausage meat wrapped around it)
Welch Rarebit (a spiced cheese sauce over toast)
Quiche (usually bacon)
Toad in the Hole (Yorkshire pudding with little link sausages)
Shepherds Pie (leftover roast beef in a gravy with mashed potatoes on top)
The meal usually ended with a pudding, which is a dessert in England.

---

fluffy scones, and served forty-three ladies a very proper afternoon tea. We were a little squished, but what a great time we had. The surprise came afterward. So many of the ladies had never been to a tea and wanted to know when we could do it again. That was many years ago, but neither of us has put the teacups away. We love sharing our homes and the delight that a tea first timer brings.

I recommend you start with a far smaller amount of guests. I once read that six guests "are a more confidence-inspiring number to serve," and that's certainly true.

While I love to read magazines with pictures of beautifully decorated homes and attractively prepared dishes and floral arrangements, it's important that we remember what hospitality is all about. Hospitality begins in our hearts. The root word comes from *hospice:* a place of shelter and healing. We can't wait to entertain until our house looks just right or has just the right dishes and silverware, or until our windows are all washed and sparkling. It's so easy to get caught up in the cares of the world and get bogged down in details. Maybe all we need is a quick pickup of clutter and little wisps with the feather duster. Keep alert for that prompting from the Holy Spirit to open your home for "hospitalitea!"

With our busy lifestyles, an afternoon tea has many advantages. Most of the food preparation can be done before the guests arrive. Only the tea needs

Boston Tea Party Cream Pie[1]

I love the look of this cake with the custard peeking out between the layers and chocolate frosting drip, dropping down the sides. First preheat oven according to package directions and get out all ingredients. Baking pans too.

The Cake
Prepare 1 box of white cake mix according to directions. Bake in two 8-inch cake pans and cool for about 10 minutes. Then remove to wire racks and cool completely before assembling the "pie."

The Custard
Mix Bird's Custard Mix (If you can't find custard mix, use one small box of vanilla pudding—cooked pudding, not the instant pudding) according to directions, plus $1/2$ tsp. real vanilla. Cool completely before filling "pie." Same directions for vanilla pudding mix.

Putting It Together
Place one cake layer on a plate, spread custard or pudding over top. You'll have a little custard left over which can be used for individual dessert cups. Place second cake layer on top, press down lightly.

Chocolate Drip-Drop Frosting
Melt 1 square unsweetened chocolate (1 oz.) and 2 tbs. butter on lowest burner setting and watch closely. Remove from heat. Add 1 cup powdered sugar and 2 tbs. boiling water and beat with electric mixer until smooth and glossy. Let mixture set for 10 minutes and then pour over top of "pie" while still warm. The frosting will seem thin but will thicken in a while. (Refrigerate cake after frosting has cooled.) And, dear baker, you can even put a cherry on top! —DOLLEY CARLSON

[1] © 2001 by Dolley Carlson, *Friendship Gifts from the Heart*. Copied with permission by Cook Communications Ministries, p. 32. May not be further reproduced. All rights reserved.

to be made just before you begin serving the food. I try to do as much as possible the week before the tea. You should plan on getting a little time to rest before everyone arrives, so you can enjoy the fruits of your labor. It's much better to have less food and fewer guests than to be a total wreck when everyone arrives. The pleasure and comfort of our visitors should be one of our top priorities.

When entering our homes, each person should feel the love of Christ. It isn't so much what we put on the table to serve, but who we are serving in the chairs.

"Therefore, as God's chosen people, holy and dearly loved, clothe yourselves with compassion, kindness, humility, gentleness, and patience" (Col. 3:12).

Planning Is the Key to Having a Lovely Tea

Planning ahead really is essential for all entertaining. Have everything ready and organized. Work backward with your time planner, and then you will know if you can make that extra dessert. I suggest if you have never given a tea, allow yourself some extra time. Keys to a successful event:

- Set the date and time for your tea.
- Make a guest list and send the invitations.
- Plan the menu and shopping list.
- Check your linens, serving dishes, silver, etc.
- Prepare as much of the food as possible in advance.
- Set the table the day before.

With the many blends of tea available from all over the world, teatime can be an exotic experience. Tea can be made with tea bags or loose-leaf tea, the latter being the preferable. Although tea bags are very popular in Britain and the world, loose-leaf tea gives a much better taste. I compare it to making coffee with brewed coffee or instant coffee granules.

Since the popularity of tea continues to grow, all the large tea merchants are marketing new blends. With so many to choose from, I would suggest you start with a traditional English tea, such as Assam, Darjeeling, Keemun, English Breakfast, or Earl Grey. These teas all have a pleasant and flavorful taste and are readily available.

Tips for Preparing Tea

- Use fresh cold water.
- Choose quality loose-leaf tea.
- Warm the teapot with hot tap water.
- Pour boiling water over the tea leaves.
- Let the tea steep for three to five minutes, no more.
- Remove the leaves from the teapot, using a tea infuser or tea ball, or use a tea strainer and pour the tea into your cup.

Serving Tea

As a rule, most of the English prefer their tea with milk. Before pouring the tea, ask your guests if they would like milk or sugar. Only use milk, not cream or half-and-half. (Milk would not be used with a fruit tea, green tea, or tisanes). Milk and the traditional sugar cubes should be added to the cup before pouring the tea. If you have never tried milk with tea, give it a whirl.

Small teaspoons are lovely to use to stir the tea. My mother had a set of "apostles" spoons that I have used for many years and now collect. They are smaller than a teaspoon, and reminded me that we could also use demitasse spoons, our children's baby spoons or the souvenir spoons we collect on vacations. One little rule of tea etiquette I need to mention here: stirring your tea should be almost silent. My grandchildren remind me of this every time we have tea.

An original set of Apostle spoons consisted of thirteen spoons, usually silver, with adorned handles representing Jesus and the twelve apostles. These silver spoons, originally produced in the 1500s, were individually made and given by the wealthy to their grandchildren or godchildren as a Christening present. Only that person would then use the spoons, and it would be kept for life.

Reproductions were much smaller, similar to a demitasse spoon and were popular wedding gifts in the 1930s and 1940s.

The basics for serving tea are very simple. If you only have a few guests, you as the hostess will pour the tea. If more than six are in attendance, ask your best friend to help you pour the tea. This is considered an honor. The person pouring the tea is referred to as the "mum," a ritual that began with Queen Victoria.

"If you are cold, tea will warm you,
If you are heated, it will cool you,
If you are depressed it will cheer you,
If you are excited, it will calm you."

—William E. Gladstone (1809–1898)

Sandwich-making Tips

- Buy sandwich or pullman loaves.
- Freeze the bread before making sandwiches.
- Have butter and cream cheese at room temperature for easy spreading.
- Mix wheat and white slices.
- Make a different shape for each type of sandwich, so as to help your guests know the kind to choose.
- Use an electric knife to trim and cut the sandwiches.
- Tie two sandwiches together with very thin ribbon for a festive look.

- Make the sandwiches ahead of time and keep them fresh by covering with damp paper towels, tea towels, or lettuce leaves. Keep them refrigerated and covered until ready to serve.

Scones

Scones are the mainstay of an English tea. They are little cakes, almost comparable to our muffins. A good basic recipe allows you to add additional ingredients without having to find new recipes. Orange juice can replace the milk for the liquid, and adding one-quarter cup of any dried fruit will make a yummy scone. They are best served warm, but can be made the day before and reheated for five to ten minutes. To eat a scone, cut it in half like

---

MOTHER'S SCONES

2 cups flour	$\frac{1}{2}$ teaspoon salt
2 teaspoons sugar	$\frac{1}{2}$ cup unsalted butter
1 teaspoon cream of tartar	$\frac{1}{2}$ cup buttermilk
1 teaspoon baking soda	

Sift dry ingredients together in a large bowl and cut in the butter with a pastry blender or two knives until the flour mixture resembles flaky crumbs. Stir in milk to form a soft dough; don't overhandle. Turn the dough out onto a lightly floured surface and pat into $\frac{3}{4}$" thickness. Cut with a floured biscuit cutter (2-2½-inch diameter), and arrange them fairly close together on a lightly greased baking sheet. Brush tops with cream and bake 12-15 minutes at 400°F until lightly golden brown. Cool 5 minutes before removing from pan. Makes 8 to 10. Serve warm with jam and Devonshire cream. You may add to the dough one of the following: grated lemon or orange zest, $\frac{1}{4}$ cup of any of the following: currants, dried apricots, cherries, cranberries or sultanas. Coat dried fruit with 2 tablespoons of flour before adding to scone mixture. Serve warm with jam and Devonshire cream.

(Mock) Devonshire Cream

$^1/_4$ cup sour cream   1   drop yellow food coloring
1   cup heavy whipping cream

Add yellow food coloring to whipping cream. Beat cream until very stiff. Gradually blend in sour cream. Serve with warm scones.

---

a hamburger bun, place jam on both halves, then top with Devonshire cream. Don't put the two halves back together.

Whether having the traditional afternoon tea for your guests, or just having a quick cup with a friend, I think you will find that teatime really does refresh your body and soul. Our desire to offer "hospitalitea" will give others a place to feel cared for and loved. Teatime can truly be an instrument in God's hands as we offer shelter and healing by sharing a cup of tea in our homes.

"And whatever you do, whether in word or deed, do it all in the name of the Lord Jesus, giving thanks to God the Father through him" (Col. 3:17).

PENELOPE CARLEVATO was born in England and came to the United States as a small child with her English mother. She resides with her husband of thirty-nine years, Norm, in Knoxville, Tennessee. They have three grown children and eight grandchildren. She is a Registered Nurse as well as a published writer and a speaker for many different types of women's organizations.

Dinner with Family, Friends, and Coworkers

Marita Littauer

AVE YOU NOTICED that food brings people together? Dinner on the table relaxes people and allows them to open up, be real, and share. It is not that the table is elegantly or perfectly set—though it may be. Nor is it that the food is fabulous and flawlessly prepared—though it may be. There is an intangible that takes place around the table. I've observed that many times a wonderful time of fellowship is being had when the host or hostess suggests, "Why don't we move into the living room where it is more comfortable?" Suddenly the ambiance changes, people look at their watch—shocked at the late hour—and declare that they must head home.

Why then, if we all agree good things happen around the table, don't we do it more often?

I remember years ago when a neighbor across the street had met a special man. She wanted to cook a nice dinner for him, and invited Chuck and me to join them. She did what many people who are not naturally gifted in the kitchen might do when faced with hosting a dinner party. She got out a variety of cookbooks and magazines and selected a menu of wonderful-sounding items with pretty pictures. When the appointed time came, we crossed the street and arrived at her house to a kitchen that was a mess, a frazzled hostess, and a late dinner. I do not know that she ever had company over for dinner again. It seemed way too much like work.

Let's look at three things that can help you make dinner with family, friends, and coworkers fun and frequent: creativity, cooking, and conversation.

Creativity

The dictionary defines the word *creative* as "resulting from originality of thought, expression, etc.; imaginative," and it is from this approach I hope you'll think with me about those special mealtimes that are shared with family and friends. I know our lives today are too busy and complex to put together a creative meal every night or a party every week, but I hope to encourage you to allow your table to be an extension of your creativity, your imaginative expression.

Invitations

When inviting guests into your home, you need to let them know about the gathering. While a phone call or e-mail works for an impromptu activity, a written invitation in the mailbox immediately feels special. Amid the bills and junk mail, there is an envelope that makes the recipient smile.

The invitation should be indicative of the type of event. A formal printed card with embossing and calligraphy advises the recipient to dress up—just like the invitation. Most of us are probably not going to be having a formal dinner party that would require that type of propriety. But we can still set the tone and build anticipation with a computer-generated invitation on an $8\frac{1}{2} \times 11$ sheet. Because I am fairly good with computer graphics, I like to play around with my invitations. I had my Bible study buddies over for a luncheon that had a Caribbean theme. I put seashells and palm trees on the invitation, using a fun font and bright colors. I used a bright-colored envelope that seemed to jump into the recipients' hands as they opened their mailboxes. Even if you're not graphically gifted, you can still create a sense of excitement through the invitation. Stores like Kinko's and Office Max have a wonderful selection of preprinted papers that set the theme for you. All you have to do is add the words by running the paper through a printer and you'll have a creative-looking invitation.

A few other things to keep in mind on your invitation include timing, menu, dress, and the guest list. Be sure that your invitation includes all the particulars: when, where, what, and who. With all of our busy schedules, it is courteous to provide a start time and an ending time so people can plan accordingly. If you intend to have appetizers for an hour and then serve the meal, indicate that on the invitation. In such an instance, I would say something like: "Hors d'oeuvres at six, dinner at seven. Please arrive sometime between six and seven, whatever fits your schedule."

Be sure to include your address and, if you have guests coming who have never been to your home, complete directions with a map. Put your phone number on the map so if your guests get lost, they have the number handy to contact you.

With all of the food allergies and different diets people are on these days, I like to include the menu on the invitation. This allows people to plan ahead or notify you if they have a food concern. For a small gathering, it would be appropriate to ask about any special food restrictions when they call to RSVP. You'd feel terrible if you prepared a prime rib and then found out most of your guests were vegetarians.

Lastly, who is coming? Are you inviting the whole family—kids and all—or is this an adults-only party. I mistakenly thought that addressing the envelope to Mr. and Mrs. indicated "adults only," until one time guests arrived with their children. It was an uncomfortable moment for everyone. At the bottom of the invitation simply state, "Please bring the whole family," or "Adults only, please."

Now that you know whom you're inviting, you need to know who is coming. The traditional way to find out this important information is by putting the letters RSVP with a phone number. However, I have discovered that many people today do not know what that really means—yet, I need to know how much food to buy and how to set the table. Therefore, I simply spell it out. At the end of the invitation, I put a line like, "To allow for proper preparation, please advise of attendance by (date). Please call (phone number) to confirm." I believe that because many people do not entertain, they do not understand the importance of the RSVP. This helps make everything clear and prevents embarrassing situations.

Table Setting

Just as an invitation creates a sense of anticipation upon its receipt, a beautiful table generates ambiance when your guests arrive. Walking in the door to a pretty table affirms that you were expecting them.

Here are some tips on table setting. Do it a day or two in advance. This is very important as it allows you to relax or take care of last-minute preparations. Plus, every time you walk by, it will make you smile and add to your excitement about the gathering.

Rather than using the good dishes for company and the everyday dishes for family, tie the table setting into the food. I have had my husband's colleagues over for a spaghetti dinner. I created a cute invitation that indicated a casual event and used my plain "restaurant white" dishes. I served a meal for just Chuck and me and used the good china. Simple sautéed chicken breasts, frozen peas, and instant mashed potatoes take on heightened status on my wedding china. Don't save the good dishes just for company and use plastic for the family—after all, who really is more important?

Because I like to entertain, I have a large collection of dishes. I have some with a nautical theme that I use for seafood. Some have a tropical flavor that I use for Mexican or Caribbean food. I have some traditional grandma-looking ones that I use for meatloaf or a casserole. If you do not have a variety of dishes, watch the after-season sales. I bought my Christmas dishes for $1.50 each at Target. Stores like Pier One or Cost Plus are also excellent sources for different dishes. I have both plain white and clear glass sets that I use for salad and dessert plates, so I only have to buy the themed dinner plates and the plain ones fill in.

Ecology is not usually my first concern, but in table settings, I am politically correct. Use placemats or a tablecloth and cloth napkins. Once you start to collect these accessories and shop the above-mentioned stores, you'll find that in the long run, they really are less expensive—and they add an easy sense of luxury. For your family, the same napkin can be used for several meals—unless it is a really messy one. On laundry day, those few extra cloth napkins hardly take up any room in the washer. They are nicer to use than paper and help the environment too!

Thank-you Notes

Many years ago I had the privilege of dining in Emilie Barnes' home. Everything was, of course, lovely. While I was still intending to write her a thank-you note, I got one in the mail from her. I was so blessed by her kindness; I determined that I was going to adopt that practice. But, I am not as organized as she is and my good intentions fell by the wayside—until I discovered a trick. I am a camera queen. I love to take pictures and keep my photo album up to date. I keep a PHD camera handy—"push here dummy." When everyone is seated, I simply get my camera, ask everyone to look my way and smile and snap the picture. When I get the film developed or the pictures printed, which could be weeks later, I send a picture to my guests with a thank you. I write something like, "I just got my pictures back. When I looked at this one of our time together, it made me smile as it brought back memories of our wonderful evening together. Thank you for joining us. It would not have been the same without you. I hope this picture makes you smile too!"

∂∽ Cooking

You've sent out invitations and set the table. Now you need to cook. (Hopefully, you already did your menu planning.)

The biggest problem people have preparing for special meals, especially those who are not naturally gifted in the kitchen, is trying too hard. Like my neighbor, many people attempt to make each aspect of the dinner a gourmet treat, using a recipe they have never tried before with a menu full of complicated and time-consuming items. This approach will leave you feeling frustrated and exhausted—and swearing you'll never cook again.

Planning

When planning a menu, I encourage people to keep it simple. If you're going to prepare a new dish that caught your eye in a current magazine, be sure everything else is easy and is something you have made successfully. For example, if you select Cornish game hens for your entrée, do simple roasted potatoes for the starch and steamed asparagus for the vegetable. For dessert, a cheesecake would be a nice complement to the fancy flair of the meal. Since cheesecake is best made a day or two in advance, it doesn't add any stress to your day.

If you're truly not comfortable in the kitchen, I recommend you use a cookbook that offers a complete meal plan, including a shopping list and timetable. In *The Godly Business Woman Magazine,* my "Tasty Sensations" column frequently features a complete meal plan. One of my favorites of this type of cookbook is called *When Entertaining.* It is now out of print, but you should be able to locate one through www.bibliofind.com. I modeled my now-out-of-print book, *HomeMade Memories,* after this cookbook.

Presentation

My father gave me an important tip for meal planning. When I was a child, he was in the restaurant business, where presentation is very important. I am sure you can think of a time when you have been in a restaurant and saw something being served to the people at the next table. You looked at it and said, "Oooh. That looks good, what is it?" The way the meal looks on the plate gets your taste buds excited in anticipation.

The tip from my father is: "Never put two foods of the same color and the same consistency on the same plate at the same time." For example, a chicken breast with a cream sauce and rice and cauliflower would all be beige. Changing the rice to a mashed sweet potato would add orange and a smooth consistency and changing the cauliflower to steamed broccoli would add green and a crisper texture—making the plate more appealing. When I am planning my menu, I always think of how it will all go together on the plate. Will it look pretty?

Of course, when you make this effort to plan a pretty plate, I suggest you serve it that way, in what is called restaurant style, not family style. Family style places platters or bowls on a table that are then passed and served—which creates extra dishes. Restaurant style is where the plate is prepared in the kitchen and presented complete—just like in a restaurant. You prepare the plates and have an older child, your spouse, or your closest friend present act as a server by carrying the plate to the table. This approach has a more formal feel and allows you to offer your guests the most pleasing presentation. Plus, it saves you having to wash those extra pieces.

Conversation

If you're not used to having guests in your home, it can feel awkward when they first arrive, especially if they do not all know each other. Here are some ideas to get the conversation flowing and to ensure that everyone has a good time.

Name Tags

If the party includes many people who do not know each other and is more of an open-house event, use name tags. But include not just the name; have people list how they know you. When I have had this type of party, I put a small table outside the front door with a sign I make up on the computer. The sign welcomes people, tells them to come on in and asks them to fill out a name tag including their name and their connection to Chuck or me. I then paste a couple sample name tags on the sign and have the name tags and markers on the table. It is amazing how that simple trick puts people at ease. Walking into a room of strangers is uncomfortable. But when you can start a conversation with someone based on his or her name tag—"I see you work with Chuck. What do you do?" "You and Marita are friends from college. Wow!"—total strangers start talking with each other.

Introductions

In a more intimate gathering where everyone may not know each other, it is your job as the hostess to introduce people to one another. I recently had a brunch where I knew everyone and most of the guests knew at least several others, but I knew there were two I had invited who probably did not know anyone but me. I made an effort to introduce these guests to others whom I specifically thought they'd find interesting—including not only their names, but also how I knew them and some other details about their lives that would provide connections for conversation.

Questions

Around the table you want the conversation to flow freely. As the hostess, you have the opportunity to steer the chatter. Again, I look to my father's guidance. When I was a child, I did not like these rules. As an adult, I totally see their value and feel frustrated when others don't operate with the benefit of my dad's training. So I pass his rules on to you. Try them, and you, too, will soon see their value.

His two dinner table conversation rules are simple:

1. Only one person talks at a time.
2. Everyone gets an equal share.

I am sure you have been at a table where several different conversations were going on—perhaps even one on each side of you. You want to listen to and participate in each, but you can't. Sometimes you may feel totally left out as others are conversing around you. At your party, you do not want anyone to be uncomfortable. To follow rule number one, steer the conversation. When several conversations get going, as the hostess, you can simply say to the second conversation participants, let's all listen to what so-and-so has to say. Doing this once or twice sets the tone and allows everyone to be involved.

Rule number two is important as some people tend to monopolize the conversation, and this rule prevents that. You do not have to announce rules; just be aware of who has not had a chance to say much and invite them into the conversation. I was recently at a dinner party where there were several of us who knew each other and were more verbose and opinionated, but one couple only knew the host. On the way home, I realized that I really knew nothing about the quieter couple. I had asked her a few questions and tried to draw her out, but he hardly said a word.

Some people are harder to draw out than others. Some people naturally join in and others need prompting. For this reason, I suggest a book called *The Book of Questions*. This simple little book has one question per page and each question is specifically designed so that it cannot be answered with "Yes" or "No" and each allows you to really get to know that person. I encourage you to flip through the book and pick three or four questions that you feel comfortable asking and keep them in your mind or on a note. When one person has taken over the conversation, at a pause, you can turn to the more quiet person and say, "Tracy, we haven't heard much from you. What do you . . . ?" Since you have already set the tone for one conversation at a time, you can easily keep the attention focused and allow that person to share—preventing one or two people from dominating the conversation.

TV

I hope it goes without saying that when you have put forth the extra effort to create a lovely atmosphere, planned a creative menu, and are aiming for stimulating conversation—whether with family, friends, or coworkers—you must turn off the TV. It kills conversation. If you're used to the noise in the background, it may seem awkward at first. So, replace the silence with pleasant music. There are many different CDs specifically designed as background music that maintain a comfortable level of volume without loud, startling sections. Find some you like, and allow the soothing music to set the stage for stimulating conversation.

I hope these tips will help you combine creativity, cooking, and conversation to make dinner with family, friends, and coworkers something that you do frequently and have fun doing.

MARITA LITTAUER is the author of thirteen books, including *But Lord, I Was Happy Shallow; Your Spiritual Personality; Personality Puzzle;* and *Talking So People Will Listen;* and is the president of CLASServices Inc., an organization that provides resources, training, and promotion for speakers and authors. Marita and her husband Chuck Noon have been married since 1983. She can be reached through www.classervices.com.

13

CHAPTER

Buffets

BETTY WINSLOW

ENTERTAINING IS tough for today's already-overbooked business-woman, who can end up exhausted before the first guest even arrives. If that's happened to you, try throwing a buffet party next time!

What exactly is a buffet, anyway? *The Woman's Day Encyclopedia* says: "BUFFET—literally translated, this French word means a 'sideboard' or 'cupboard.' In French culinary language, a buffet indicates a good-sized tiered table on which various dishes have been arranged in a decorative manner. . . . In America, the word *buffet* is used as a term for a meal where the guests help themselves from a table on which the foods are placed in a decorative array."[1]

Let's see: you can get ready much earlier, so there's less work the day of the party. You can invite more guests, since buffets don't require table seating. And, buffets run from disposable dishes and finger foods to elegant china on linen-draped tables, from a complete meal to a dessert buffet of goodies in tiny guilt-free portions. What's not to love?

---

[1] *The Woman's Day Encyclopedia*, vol. 3 (CBS Publications, 1979), pg. 46.

✒ Planning Ahead

Successful parties require lots of preplanning. Here are some things to consider:

Scheduling

This can be tricky, especially around Christmas when calendars bulge with parties, programs, family gatherings, and church events. Still, it's worth it. Holidays and special events do provide ready-made party themes—if you can just find a day and time when the majority of your desired guests don't already have plans.

Impossible? Give an open house, so guests with several events to attend can come and go as they like. Maybe they won't stay as long as you'd like, but isn't a short visit better than a no-show because of other commitments?

Consider all the angles. A Christmas Eve party may be fine for singles or married couples without children, but parents want to be home with their kids (and the bike that needs assembling once the kids are asleep). Instead, parents may enjoy a Valentine's Day party, leaving a sitter with the kids so they can concentrate on romance for an evening. Sometimes, a party only works if the special event is the centerpiece. Football fans will flock to your Super Bowl party if there's a big-screen TV and lots of finger foods.

Whom to Invite

Buffets may inspire you to invite a lot of people, but don't get carried away. A jam-packed party was proclaimed a "crush" in the eighteenth century (the highest compliment a hostess back then could receive), but modern guests already spend enough time being jostled in crowds and standing in line. People fighting traffic to get to your party don't want to fight it in your house, too.

Mix people carefully. Putting rabid Republicans and deep-dyed Democrats together is risky unless they can discuss differences amicably (or unless you enjoy raised voices). And friends who start fighting the minute they see each other should not be asked to the same party. Instead, have two parties, one following the other (to get maximum benefit from preparation), and split your guest list into compatible groups.

Parties consisting exclusively of coworkers (even with spouses) often end up all shoptalk. Throw in guests who have nothing to do with work: the neighbor who carves ice sculptures; the woman from your gym who is always reading something interesting; or your best friend from college who can always make people laugh. Your coworkers (and their spouses) will thank you.

Location

A party doesn't have to be at your house. You can rent a hall or other facility if your guest list is large and your house tiny, or give a backyard party in nice weather. If the party is at your house, consider whether you have the space necessary for a proper buffet.

Whatever you decide, make sure to choose a location that is appropriate for the guest list, the time of year, and the entertainment that you're planning. For example, the aforementioned Super Bowl party might work better in a rented hall, with a super-sized TV rented for the day, while the Valentine's Day party would work great hosted at your house, offering private corners for whispered conversations.

Food

Plan foods around the season, the party's theme, and dishes your guests enjoy. Hearty soups and casseroles, with bread hot from the bread machine, warm up winter parties; salads, cold meats, iced drinks, and an ice cream machine cranking away are perfect for sweltering summer days. Chili goes well with football—and what's Valentine's Day without at least one gooey dessert?

Save money by serving what's on sale or in season. Offer a seafood casserole instead of shrimp, or ham sandwiches in place of roast beef. For really tight times, give a potluck buffet and ask guests to bring something. If you have very cooperative friends, be specific:

"Bring an entrée that feeds six."
"Bring that artichoke dip you made at last year's office party."

Remember to consider circumstances before requesting assistance. An unemployed friend probably shouldn't be asked to bring an entrée, while a notorious non-cook won't want to bring a homemade dessert. Perhaps a six-pack of pop instead?

Afraid a potluck will make you look cheap? Ask yourself: If circumstances were reversed, would you be upset if someone asked you to bring something? No? Trust your friends to feel the same way.

Preparing for the Party

Cleaning

If time allows, clean thoroughly (or hire someone else to). Dust, mop, vacuum, polish windows, spit-shine the bathroom—the whole nine yards. However, if (like me) you can't quite pull that off, ask yourself: When the guests start arriving, will they really notice—or remember—the spotted carpet or the dusty picture frames? Nope. What they will notice is how glad you are to see them. And what they'll remember is what a great party it was and how much fun they had.

So, scrub the bathroom and entryway, tidy up the party rooms (stashing things in closets and under beds, if necessary, until tomorrow's cleanup), and empty the coat closet. Dim the lights, put on some great party music, and light scented candles (in safe, out-of-the-way places). Set out the food and it's party time!

Food

Keeping day-of-the-party food preparation to a minimum enables you to spend time getting yourself and your home ready instead of slaving in the kitchen. Your small appliance collection comes in handy here—Crock-Pot soup, bread machine bread, icy blender drinks made from a mix stashed in the freezer. Is your refrigerator too small? Ask a neighbor or family member to store nonparty food (condiments and so on) until after the party. Or rent a dorm-sized refrigerator for additional party food space.

Consider seating arrangements while menu planning. Unless all your guests will be at tables, avoid food that needs cutting or other manipulation. Instead of steak, serve thinly sliced roast beef for building sandwiches; substitute crab puffs for crab legs. For best results, buffet food should be fork or finger ready. And if it doesn't look as good as it tastes, skip it. Buffet food needs to be attractive.

Worry-Free Eggnog

Homemade eggnog, rich with egg and cream and smelling of rum, used to be a party hit, but modern concerns about possible salmonella contamination make it a big no-no to eat or drink anything that contains raw egg.

If serving store-bought eggnog doesn't appeal to you, try this Eggnog Royale recipe which offers eggnog flavor without the worry. The recipe can easily be doubled or tripled, unlike many old-time eggnog recipes, and it can be enjoyed by young or old.

EGGNOG ROYALE

1 quart softened French vanilla ice cream	1½ teaspoons freshly ground nutmeg
2 cups milk	Optional for garnish:
2 teaspoons eggnog extract (rum extract can also be added)	whipped cream & additional nutmeg

Stir softened ice cream, milk, extract, and nutmeg together in chilled punch bowl. Garnish and serve. Keep the eggnog chilled by placing punch bowl inside a slightly larger bowl filled with ice cubes or by floating ice cubes made from the Eggnog Royale recipe in the bowl.

Organization

Plan ahead to avoid traffic jams. If the serving table and eating areas are in different rooms, set up the food on the side of the room opposite the door, so people with filled plates can leave easily. If there's room, speed things up by placing the serving table parallel to, but away from the wall, with dishes accessible from both sides. Or put a long table against the wall, with identical foods leading out from the center to both ends. You can even set up identical serving tables in different areas.

Mark the starting point with a stack of plates—large enough for lots of food—or better yet, tray-plates designed especially for buffets with molded spots for a cup and extra space for silverware and food. They make buffet eating much easier for your guests—and your rug. Disposables should be sturdy enough for one-handed holding, even after filling.

Entrées come next, followed by side dishes, salads, breads, and the sauces, dips, and spreads you're serving. Make the arranged food look good—use tiered serving dishes, cake pedestals, cloth-draped boxes or crates, or large baskets. Fill extra space with flowers, candles in tip-proof holders, or knickknacks.

Napkins can go by the plates or at the end of the line, alongside silverware—chosen after your food, when you know what you need. Napkins and silverware can also be rolled into neat little packages tied with colorful ribbons, for easy grabbing. In that case, provide extra napkins and silverware for guests who need them.

Place beverages and desserts at the very end of the table, on another table entirely, or even in a different room which might prevent traffic jams caused by people going back for coffee or another piece of pie. If you do place the desserts and beverages away from the main table, put extra silverware and napkins there too.

Punch bowls are pretty but messy. Mix your punch recipe in the kitchen and transfer it to pitchers for easier pouring. If you must have a punch bowl, waterproof the table and provide a ladle with a pouring lip on each side—it *does* make a difference.

Serve coffee in thermal carafes marked Regular and Decaf—and do provide both. If your guests are tea drinkers, put out a carafe of hot water and some tea bags. In cold weather, supply envelopes of hot chocolate and instant spiced cider. In hot weather, it's still okay to serve hot drinks—coffee and tea lovers drink it year-round—but add pitchers of something cool, like lemonade or unsweetened tea. I know my Southern relatives may protest, but unsweetened tea allows guests to drink tea the way they like it—with or without sugar or sweetener.

Provide strategically placed empty spaces along the serving tables where guests can set plates down while buttering rolls or sugaring coffee. Provide a small waste container for empty sugar packets, used tea bags, and so on. And empty it from time to time.

Helping Hands

Helpers can refill serving dishes and ice buckets, make punch and coffee, hang up or fetch coats, empty trash cans, and bus dirty dishes, allowing you to mingle and make sure everyone is having fun. You do have helpers, don't you? You should. How about a young relative who'd like to make a few extra dollars? Or the teenager down the street? You can guarantee successful assistance with a pre-party training session to show helpers where everything is and

---

TO SPEED THINGS UP

Refill ice buckets fast with gallon-sized zippered plastic bags of ice. Switch empty serving dishes with full ones snatched from the refrigerator. Place premeasured ground coffee into filters stacked next to the coffee maker. Line each trash can (there should be several) with several bags, one inside the other. Full bags can be removed and tossed leaving clean ready-to-use ones behind.

how you want things done. Be sure to post instructions—how to make coffee, where dirty dishes and trash go, and so on.

Food Safety

Food poisoning is not fun. Be sure to wash hands well before preparing food and keep preparation areas squeaky clean. Handle hot and cold foods with care to avoid foodborne illness. Or, to skip potential problems altogether, serve food that tastes good and is safe to eat at room temperature. Put serving tongs or silverware in each serving dish. Clearly label foods containing potentially serious allergens, such as shellfish, peanuts, and strawberries. And don't serve anything that contains raw egg. (See page 125 for a party-friendly eggnog recipe that contains no eggs and no alcohol.) Allow guests time to wash up before dinner.

To avoid sending your guests home with a nasty case of food poisoning, be sure to keep hot foods hot and cold foods cold. According to the U.S. FDA, disease-causing bacteria grow best in temperatures between 40 and 140 degrees Fahrenheit and any cooked food that has been in this range for more than two hours should be disposed of. (Check out the U. S. FDA's Center for Food Safety and Applied Nutrition for more information on how you can make food safety a part of every event: http://www.cfsan.fda.gov/list.html.)

If a buffet dish is to be served hot, heat it immediately before serving or serve from a dish kept hot over boiling water, a Crock-Pot, a warming pan, or another direct source of heat.

Cold foods should be kept in the refrigerator until just before serving and kept chilled on the table in a bed of ice or an insulated dish. To reduce the chances of foodborne illness, split servings up, keeping the backup food chilled or heating until needed. Make sure your guests take home good memories from your next buffet, not bad bacteria.

Guests on Special Diets

If you know you'll be entertaining guests on special diets, offer things they can eat, marked accordingly—Low Sodium, Vegan, Fat-Free. My extended family comes over every Christmas Eve for a buffet dinner. This year, we've added five newly minted vegetarians. For their convenience and to warn the confirmed meat-and-potato eaters, I'm inserting colored frilled toothpicks into dishes they can eat.

At work, my coworkers and I mark dairy-free dishes for our lactose-intolerant coworker. If a guest needs to know a dish's ingredients, will you remember them all? Be prepared—post your recipes on a bulletin board hung by the serving table, with extra copies for interested guests. This also saves you from forgetting to whom you promised to send a recipe.

Seating

Will your guests sit or stand as they eat? You don't have to provide chairs at a table for everyone, but having a few available for older guests is thoughtful. The rest can make do with TV or lap trays, card tables, floor cushions (for the younger or more flexible), and folding chairs next to coffee or end tables—cleared of knickknacks and provided with coasters. Allow space for room traffic—getting up and down and maneuvering around the table.

Keep a Party Journal

Write down the details after each party: Menu. Recipes and amounts used. Guests invited. Decorations. Add comments: So-and-so was a great helper. We ran out of punch. The spinach quiche bombed. Do this after every party and before long, you'll be known for your great buffets. Buffet parties really are the solution for busy women who want to entertain. Throw one soon, and let the good times roll!

Ohioan BETTY WINSLOW, a confirmed writer, has contributed to many magazines, Web sites, and anthologies. Betty and Mark have been married thirty-two years and have two daughters, two sons, and one granddaughter. Betty loves reading, writing, crocheting, baking, and singing. She can be reached at freelancer@wcnet.org.

Children's Parties

RHONDA WEBB

Remind me—why are all these urchins in my yard? Who are they? Why are they pulling up my flowers?"

Children's parties? Oh my!

We plan them with only the best intentions of creating festive, fun, and cherished memories for our kids. But before the party is over, the grown-ups are just hoping for survival. There *is* a way to create a most delightful and memorable party for your child, one at which the kids and you have a lot of fun. It just takes a plan—one that includes basic logistics, theme, invitations, scheduled activities, food, and favors.

That plan is the most important element of your child's party. Three or four weeks before the big event, sit down and commit your plan to paper. You must write it down. Just thinking about it won't guarantee success.

Basic Logistics

Date and Time

For kids, afternoons are best, and weekend afternoons are the best of all. You will need a block of time—no more than two hours and no less than ninety minutes.

Place

You can choose from a plethora of locations for your event. Your home, a skating rink, bowling alley, a fast-food restaurant, or party venues are just a few of your options. If you choose to hold the party at your home, strongly consider a theme or strategy that lets you celebrate outdoors. A number of excited kids inside your home is often a recipe for disaster.

Theme

Why have a theme? Trust me—it's essential to your sanity. A theme helps you maintain focus and keeps your activities from being too diverse for the children to enjoy. Kids also love telling their friends, "I'm having a _____ Party."

The words that fill in that blank are as limitless as the stars in the sky: Cowboy, Campout, Scooby-Doo, Mystery, Bowling, Dog, Tea, Glamour Girl, Beach. How about picking your child's favorite color and having a Pink Party or a Purple Party?

Sit down with your child and ask him to throw out some ideas of the kind of party he would like. Present some ideas of your own. Then come to a consensus, and stick to it.

PARTY THEME IDEAS

- Cowboy Party
- Campout Party
- Mystery Party
- Glamour Girl Party
- Bowling Party

- Treasure Hunt Party
- Princess Party
- Tea Party
- Pink Party

Invitations

Before you send out invitations, determine how many kids you can feasibly accommodate considering your location and other resources. A good rule for birthday parties is to invite the number of children equal to the number of years being celebrated.

When having a children's party, the old saying, "the more the merrier," absolutely does *not* apply. Some women believe they need to invite a child's entire class so feelings are spared. Those are the folks who afterwards swear they will never have another party. Your child will accept the rule if you present it to him as: "You're seven, so you can invite seven friends to your party." He will only remember his closest friends being there anyway, and setting a limit helps him prioritize. It also helps you avoid inviting known trouble-makers—a *must* for party survival.

Once you're settled on the number of guests and whom the list will include, it's time to get to work on the invitations. On each, indicate for whom the party is being held, date, time (starting and ending), place, and a request for an RSVP. It really helps your child to know who will and will not be attending, so he is not disappointed on the day of the party.

Before you mail the invitations, make a list of the invitees and their parents' names and telephone numbers. If you haven't heard from them at least three days before the event, give them a ring and ask if the child will be attending. This is totally acceptable. Invitations do get lost in the mail, and parents of young children do sometimes forget to respond. But it is important for you to know the exact number of favors, cups, and so forth you will need.

Mail the invitations two to three weeks before the event. Do not deliver them at school; the children who are not invited may be hurt.

Scheduled Activities

A schedule is required. Plan every single minute of your child's party with activities. Do *not* plan time for dropping off and picking up. Your schedule should include one main activity, one or two busy activities, a game, time to eat, and time to open gifts.

Dropping Off

Although you need not schedule time for dropping off, a few words are warranted. If at all possible, do not allow parents to stay. Tell them you can manage, and to enjoy the break. Ask a friend or two—preferably no relation to any attendees—or a few high school or college kids to help you during the party. Kids have more fun and better behavior at parties when their parents are not present. Expect younger siblings to filter in. Plan for extra kids just in case Bobby's younger brother happens to stick around for the festivities. Better to be prepared and gracious than to experience the drama of Bobby's mother prying Little Johnny's knuckles from the door as he screams at the top of his lungs.

Main Activity

Your main activity should be in keeping with your theme. If you're having a Cowboy Party, have ponies. If you're having a Glamour Girl Party, give manicures with all different colors of polish, dots, flowers, and stripes. For a Knight Party, have a jumping castle. For a Mystery Party, create a mystery. For a Campout Party, make plans for a hayride or a campfire.

Busy Activities

Plan one or two activities that fill time. When a few of the girls are getting polka dots painted on their toes, the others can be stringing beads for necklaces that they get to take home. While some are riding ponies, others can be jumping into a giant leaf pile—the most successful busy activity at my son's birthday parties. If time permits, the children can revisit these activities while waiting for their parents to pick them up.

Games

You can plan games into your party—just don't plan more than one or two. More will make the kids feel rushed and shuffled around. Don't forget the old standards like pin the tail on the donkey and breaking a piñata. If the games get too complex, the kids lose interest.

Time to Eat

Include time in your schedule to eat cake or whatever goodies you have prepared. This usually takes no more than ten to fifteen minutes.

Opening gifts

Have a table or basket for the gifts. When the children arrive, have them put their gift in the designated place and tell them that the gifts will be opened all at one time, later in the party. Schedule time for opening gifts before eating time. Have the kids sit in a circle. You can even have each retrieve his or her gift before sitting in the circle and spin the bottle" to determine the order in which the gifts will be opened. Tell the kids that after all the presents are opened, it will be time for cake. That's powerful motivation for sitting quietly while the birthday boy or girl opens gifts.

SAMPLE SCHEDULES

Jimmy's Cowboy Party

2:30 P.M.—Check: tables, plates, napkins, cups, cake, drinks, craft stuff, sharpie marker, ponies, hats, and bandanas.

3:00 P.M.—Kids arrive, put gifts in red wagon, put on cowboy hats and bandanas and start stringing beads. Daddy and Jimmy greet guests. Mommy and Helper help kids with hats/bandanas, write names on bandanas and in hats, and get kids started making necklaces/bracelets.

Yippee-ki-yea! Jimmy is 4!
It's a Roundup!

Saddlin' up at 4:00 p.m.
Saturday, November 4th.

Rockin' W Ranch - 3987 Silverlake

We'll corral the ponies then we'll be
cookin' up some grub 'round the
campfire.

Headin' out about 6:30 p.m.

Ya'll come!
An' give us a holler at 333-6898!

3:20 P.M.—Pony rides.

Kids not riding ponies can string beads or jump in the leaf pile.

Mom: stay at bead table.

Dad: manage pony rides.

Helper: play in leaf pile.

4:00 P.M.—Hayride. Dad drives tractor. Helper rides with kids. Mom gets food ready.

4:20 P.M.—Open presents around picnic table. Dad is in charge of trash.

4:30 P.M.—Eat cowboy cake and drink cactus juice at picnic table.

String beads and play in leaves until parents come. Mommy and helper manage activities. Daddy and Jimmy make sure kids take home their hats and bandanas and say thank you to guests and parents as they leave.

Abby's Glamour Girl Party

1:30 P.M.—Check: table, plates, napkins, cups, cake, drinks, beads, foam frame stuff, manicure table, dress-up box, music, flip-flops at front door, gift table, party favors.

2:00 P.M.—Girls arrive, put gifts on table by door, put on flip-flops and begin making sparkly beaded necklaces. Mom and Abby stand at the door. Helper One stays at the table helping with necklaces. Helper Two takes gifts, writes girls' names on bottom of flip-flops, and assists Helper One.

2:15 P.M.—Manicures/pedicures by Mom and Helper One.

While waiting for manicures, girls, with Helper Two's help, get started making foam picture frames.

3:00 P.M.—Glamour shots with Polaroid. Pull out the dress-up box and have girls pose for pictures. Make sure each girl has a photo with the birthday girl to take home in her frame. Play music and let the girls have a dance while

waiting on photos. Take lots of pictures of them dancing and dressing up. Mom takes pictures. Helper One and Two dance and help girls dress up.

3:20 P.M.—Gather girls around coffee table to open gifts.

Mom writes down gifts. Helper One and Two prepare cake and ice cream.

3:30 P.M.—Have birthday cake and ice cream.

3:40 P.M.—Finish putting frames together with pictures. Dance until parents come.

Send girls home with flip-flops and pictures. Helper One and Two dance and work on frames while Mom and Abby pass out favors and thank guests and parents.

Food and Favors

Food

For easier serving during the party, consider cupcakes or even cookies instead of birthday cake. Have the food coincide with your theme. For a Dog Party, have bone-shaped cookies. For a Tea Party, have a teakettle-shaped cake. Include a fun drink; for example, for a Cowboy Party, have Gatorade and call it cactus juice. For a Beauty Parlor or Princess Party, the punch must be pink—and of course, it is called Princess Punch. Pass out the drinks in plastic tumblers that fit your theme. The kids can take their cup with them as a party favor.

Sometimes—although very rarely—a whole meal makes sense. For a Cowboy or Campout Party, have a campfire for roasting hot dogs and marshmallows. For a girls' party, serve finger sandwiches cut with cookie cutters into flower or heart shapes. Just keep it simple. Pizza is a perfect option, especially if you can have it delivered at just the right time!

Favors

If at all possible, send the children home with *no* candy. Their parents will appreciate it. Think of inexpensive toys that go along with the theme of your

---

BIRTHDAY PARTY RESOURCES

- Birthday in a Box (800) 989-5506 www.birthdayinabox.com
- Birthday Express (800) 424-7843 www.birthdayexpress.com
- Birthday Party Ideas "Big List of Kid's Party Ideas" www.birthdaypartyideas.com

---

child's party: tumblers, flip-flops, straw cowboy hats, bandanas, flashlights, pencils, and so on. Put favors in sealed party bags tagged with each child's name and have them waiting at the front door—if the kids aren't wearing them. The children can pick them up on their way out.

Conclusion

Making a written-out, detailed plan is the key to maintaining your composure and your sanity during a children's party. It is also quite helpful in assuring that the children have a great time.

Enlist your child's help in creating the plan. She can help you come up with fun activities and games, and tell you what would be the best kind of cake.

You can use your child's party as a tool to teach him wonderful life lessons:

- Organization
- Participation
- Patience
- Imagination
- Hospitality
- Gratitude

During the party, the most important thing to remember besides the plan is to *participate*. It is so much more fun for the kids when the adults act silly and play along. Dress up. Dress like a dog for a Dog Party. Wear boots and a

> "Train a child in the way he should go, and when he is old he will not turn from it." (Prov. 22:6)

hat for a Cowboy Party. Dress up like a manicurist from the movie *Legally Blonde* for your daughter's Glamour Girl Party. Wear camouflage for a campout. If it is a Bowling Party, then bowl. Don't just watch. You will be modeling a very important behavior for your child that being a participant is more fun than being a bystander. You both should jump in with both feet and have fun!

Take lots of pictures. If you're going to go to all this trouble, you want your kids to at least be able to look back and see how awesome the party was when they are old enough to truly appreciate it.

Finally, have your child write thank-you notes as early as he is able to write. If he can only write his name, ask him to tell you what to write in the note and then let him sign his name.

RHONDA WEBB is a popular speaker at conferences and retreats, and the author of *Words Begin in Our Hearts: What God Says about What We Say* (Moody). She has a passion for antiques, decorating, and entertaining. Rhonda, her husband, Jim, and their children, Jimmy and Scout, enjoy their country home in Oklahoma.

Festive Parties Your Teen Will Love

GENA MASELLI

P LANNING A PARTY for your teen is a fun and creative experience. No, really—it is! With a little planning and the right connections, you'll have the satisfaction of giving your teen a special memory. So, get imaginative. Get innovative and get ready. You're about to plan an event that will be remembered as a family favorite for years!

Get the Ball Rolling

Being a busy woman, things like planning a party for your teen can sneak up on you if you don't prepare. The best way to prevent this is to put a reminder in your daily planner or calendar two months before the special day.

On that day, begin making a list of things that need to be accomplished and when, then you won't be overwhelmed as the big day draws closer. Treat the party like every other important project in your schedule, and you'll keep your stress level to a minimum and help ensure a smoothly run event. When the big day arrives, your teen will realize just how special he or she is because of the care you gave the party planning.

Teen Party Planning To-do List

Your party to-do list should include:

- Choose party day
- Talk with your teen's friend or sibling to help plan the party
- Choose the type of invitation—e-mail, written, phone call
- Send invitations
- Order bakery items
- Shop for food
- Send reminder to invitees
- Ask the teen to set up online wish lists for gifts
- Order decorations
- Order gift

Don't Go It Alone

You know the power of delegation in the business world. You know that the best managers are the ones who know how to draw from others' strengths and incorporate those strengths into the big picture. In other words, you don't try to do everything yourself. The same is true when planning a great party—especially for your teen.

Of course, if you're planning a party that isn't a surprise, include your teen in the theme decision. But what if it *is* a surprise party?

"The best teen parties are the ones that the teens create themselves," Jennifer Ryan, Co-Youth Pastor at Riverwalk Fellowship in Haltom City, Texas, says. Since you may not know all your teen's closest friends or the latest trends, why not turn to someone who does? Draft a teenage sibling or one of your teen's friends to help plan the party. He or she will know your teen's tastes and friends and the latest and greatest in cool party ideas. This person can help you put together the guest list, keep track of the RSVPs, choose a party theme, plan the menu, and decorate on the day of the party.

That doesn't mean that you don't need to be involved. After all, slave labor *is* illegal. But it will take the pressure off of you having to do everything yourself. Plus, the party will be more to your teen's liking, and you'll have the opportunity to get to know your teen's friends and tastes.

Dream Themes

Do you remember the line from the movie *Field of Dreams:* "If you build it, they will come?" Well, in the same way, if you pick the right theme for the party, the rest of the ideas, creativity, and partygoers *will come.* Picking a theme for your teen's party can help you decide on the decorations, invitations, food, and dress code. It'll set the whole course of the party.

Obviously, you want to decide on a theme that will interest your teen. Don't throw a barbecue if he or she hates the outdoors. And don't plan a party at a Japanese steak house, if your teen only likes hamburgers and pizza. This isn't the time to expand his or her horizons. Save new experiences for another time unless your teen likes the unexpected.

Here are a few party themes to consider:

A Night with the Stars

Make it a red carpet evening if your teen likes to dress up. Ask guests to come as their favorite Hollywood stars—evening gowns, wild costumes, and anything else their creative minds can create. As a fun addition to the evening, consider rolling out your own red carpet for guests to walk down.

'70s Party

Believe it or not, the '70s are back. Teens are intrigued by fun, quirky customs from the days of *Saturday Night Fever*. For decorations, get funky. Think lava lamps, disco balls, and big smiley faces. Consider having the guests dress for the '70s—bell-bottoms, Qiana polyester shirts, and so on. Or, make it a '60s or '80s party.

Luau Party

This theme presents a nice twist on the standard barbecue. The décor can include paper lanterns, tiki torches, and leis. Throw in a bonfire for cooking hamburgers, hot dogs, and marshmallows, and you're set.

Country and Western Theme

Dust off those Tony Lamas and don those Stetsons. What better way to kick off the fall than with a hoedown? Decorating is as easy as scattering hay on the ground and placing bales of hay for seating. Throw in a bonfire with roasted marshmallows and you have a recipe for a fun party.

Winter Wonderland

This idea is especially good if you live in an area that doesn't see snow often. Teens can get involved in the decorating and let their imaginations run wild. Start with your Christmas tree. Add confetti or white fiberfill, which you can find in craft and quilting stores, for fake snow. Ask the guests to wear warm sweaters, and serve hot chocolate while the teens listen to Christmas music or watch classic Christmas movies.

Irresistible Invitations

Creating invitations for a teen's party may seem like a daunting task, but don't worry—it's easier than you think. Since most teens are technologically savvy, why not send an e-invitation? They're easy—and free!

There are several online party invitation sites. You'll want to visit a few, but www.evite.com is a good place to begin your search. This party-planning site will give you lots of design styles so you can find the right one for your theme. In addition to sending out invitations, eVite.com and similar sites include response keys on the electronic invitation for RSVPs so that you can track who has accepted or declined the invitations. Of course, you'll want to call or e-mail those who haven't responded to the invitation a few days before the party to get an accurate count and make sure they received the invitation.

When deciding whom to invite to your teen's party, you'll probably want to steer away from mixing family and friends unless the family members are close to the teen's age. Most teens won't want their grandparents, aunts, and uncles mixing in a party with their school friends.

Puttin' on the Dawg

Though you may be a detail-oriented perfectionist in the business world, remember that when throwing a teen party, it's more about the people than the decorations or the menu. As fun, creative, social creatures, teens are sure to entertain themselves regardless of whether you've spent fifty or five hundred dollars.

If you need to order decorations, make it simple for yourself and order online. By visiting Web sites like www.ThemePartiesNMore.com and www.iParty.com, you can find great accessories to highlight your teen's party. These sites will even have decoration ideas based on party themes.

Fantastic Food

When it comes to teens and food, it just doesn't get any easier to choose the menu. For many teens, if you plan American fast food—hamburgers, hot dogs, and pizza—you have a winning menu. For those who might be health conscious, you could include sliced veggies, baked chips, and even lemon slices for ice water. If you want to get creative, consider one of these alternatives:

Flavored Popcorn

This is a hot trend among young people. You can choose from different flavors of cheese or fruit popcorn and popcorn toppings. You'll find flavored popcorn at grocery stores or stores like Target and Wal-Mart.

Ice Cream Sundaes

With a few basic flavors of ice cream and an assortment of toppings, teens will have fun creating their own sundaes. Consider serving toppings like nuts, maraschino cherries, whipped toppings, sliced fruit, coconut, chocolate and caramel syrups, and anything else that looks yummy.

Fondue

Believe it or not, fondue is making a comeback. By providing things like bread and veggies to dip in a cheese fondue and marshmallows and fruit to dip in a chocolate fondue, you're sure to create a fun party memory for your teen. For Sally Hall, an avid teen party planner, fondue parties are always a hit. Here are a few of Sally's recipes that you're sure to enjoy.

SALLY HALL'S THREE-CHEESE FONDUE

1¼ cups cooking wine, divided	8 ounces Goat cheese
2 teaspoon cornstarch	Nutmeg
2 teaspoon lemon juice	White pepper
1 clove minced garlic	2 tablespoon chopped parsley
8 ounces Raclette or Gouda cheese	Cubed French, Italian, or
8 ounces Garlic-pepper	other bread
Monterey Jack cheese (or other	
Monterey Jack cheese)	

In a small mixing bowl, pour ¼ cup cooking wine and cornstarch. Stir until smooth and set aside. In a saucepan on the stove, bring 1 cup cooking wine and lemon juice to a boil. Add 1 clove of minced garlic. Gradually add Raclette, Garlic-pepper Monterey Jack, and Goat cheese. Stir constantly until mixture is smooth. Stir in the cornstarch mixture, continue stirring, and bring to a boil. Season to taste with nutmeg and white pepper. Add parsley. Pour cheese into heated fondue pot. Serve with large cubes of bread for dipping.

SALLY'S CHOCOLATE FONDUE

1 cup heavy cream (or half and half)	Assorted sliced fruit, including oranges, apples, pineapple, pears, grapes, etc.
1 tablespoon orange zest	
$\frac{1}{4}$ cup orange juice	Marshmallows
Pinch of salt	Chopped coconut
8 ounces semi-sweet chocolate	Chopped nuts

In a saucepan or fondue pot, heat heavy cream (or half and half) with orange zest, orange juice, and salt. Add 8 ounces of semi-sweet chocolate, stirring constantly over low heat until completely melted and smooth. Pour mixture into the fondue pot and serve.

To add an extra treat, serve fondue with a side bowl of coconut or chopped nuts to roll the fruit and marshmallows in after they've been dipped in chocolate.

Gifts and Presents

If the party you're planning includes presents, wish lists at online stores are just the thing to make your life easier. Instead of keeping track of what your teen wants and where to get it, ask him or her to register online. Amazon.com has a system that is free, fun, and easy to use. After your teen has registered online, he or she simply indicates items for a wish list. Amazon.com is connected to a wide variety of other merchants, including clothing stores, hobby stores, athletic stores, electronic stores, and more.

Then, as people visit the list, they simply click the "Buy It" button and order the item online. Amazon.com will record that the item has already been purchased so that your teen doesn't receive duplicates. When your teen signs on to his or her wish list, it will only show what was originally included in the list, not what has been purchased, so his or her gifts will remain a surprise.

With a little planning, assistance from a teen helper, and an Internet connection, you can give your teen a party he or she won't forget. By using online stores and party planner sites, you won't be limited to the norm. No, you'll be able to plan a party that's creative, unusual, and fun—all from the comfort of your home or office.

Above Board

When planning parties for teens, it's important to have adults involved. Even the best-behaved Christian kids can get into questionable territory if left unsupervised. Jennifer Ryan, Co-Youth Pastor at Riverwalk Fellowship in Haltom City, Texas, has suggestions for making your teen's party wholesome.

- Make sure the invitees know it is a Christian party in a nonthreatening and non-preachy way.
- Don't watch movies with questionable content.
- Establish a dress code in advance.
- Provide a Christian-related party favor, something that will minister to nonbelievers.
- Keep track of conversations and interrupt conversations that sound ungodly.

GENA MASELLI lives in Fort Worth, Texas, with her family and their two feline friends. She is the author of *Truth Unplugged for Boys* and *Truth Unplugged for Girls* and the co-author of *Daily Wisdom for Working Women*.

16

CHAPTER

Engagement Parties

Michelle Medlock Adams

YOU'RE ENGAGED. OK! Now the real fun begins—planning the wedding, choosing the all-important dress, and attending a plethora of parties. While you won't be throwing most of your upcoming prenuptial parties, you will be involved in planning many of them—especially the engagement party. It's the very first party on the list, and it's one of the most important.

Traditionally, the parents of the bride host the party to announce the engagement of their daughter. However, as times change, it's also acceptable for the groom's parents or a close friend or sibling to host the party.

Don't get stressed. It will be a fun, easy activity. Just think of it this way— this is simply a celebratory gathering so that you can share the exciting news with a few close friends and relatives. Just do the following do's and avoid the don'ts, and you'll be on your way to an awesome and enjoyable engagement party.

Don't Overdo

If you're like most women, you've dreamed of your wedding day since you were a little girl with pigtails. You've dressed up in your mother's pearls and high heels and hummed the wedding march as you sashayed down the hallway in your childhood home. You've planned your wedding day down to the very last detail. You've collected ideas and clipped magazine articles, all in preparation for your upcoming wedding. That's good, but don't waste all of your good stuff on the engagement party. If you do, you'll have nothing spectacular left for the actual wedding day. Of the two events, your wedding day is by far the more important. Make your engagement party nice, but not as nice as the main event!

Don't Over Invite

Before deciding on the engagement party guest list, it's wise to sit down with your fiancé and come up with a tentative guest list for your wedding. You won't want to invite anyone to your engagement party that you won't be inviting to the actual wedding. Remember, the engagement party is simply that—a party. It doesn't have to be a formal occasion. Keep it small and intimate and celebrate this joyful time with only your closest friends and family members.

Do Invite in Style

Many brides-to-be feel pressured to order formal invitations for the engagement party, but that really isn't necessary. Let the tone of your event set the tone of your invitation. If you're simply having twenty friends over to your home for a barbecue, it's perfectly okay to e-mail or call your guests and invite them. Or, for a more creative touch, why not make your invitations, playing up the barbecue theme? For instance, you might use red-and-white checked ribbons to adorn the invitations.

You might want to use formal invitations if your event is being hosted at a hotel or restaurant where an RSVP is required. This same rule applies if you're using a caterer that needs an exact head count for your event.

Do Provide Gift Ideas

If you're hosting a more formal event, guests will know to bring presents. That's a good thing; however, it's not so good if they bring gifts that you don't want or can't return. Of course, you should always be gracious even if you've opened seventeen waffle irons in a row. Help your guests by registering at a few of your favorite shops. Or, simply provide your mother and your future mother-in-law with a gift wish list. Guests often call on them for gift ideas, so give them some ammunition.

If you're hosting a more casual affair, many guests may not bring gifts or may stick to something small and sentimental. Never expect a gift, and graciously accept all with a smile. If you would rather not receive gifts, simply include that preference on your invitation. Some friends and family may still bring gifts, but at least they won't feel obligated to do so.

Don't Stress over Location

No matter where you hold your engagement party, it's sure to be a success as long as you plan ahead. Traditionally, the parents of the bride-to-be will host the engagement party at their house or at a location of their choosing. If your parents' home is large enough to accommodate your guest list and they agree—go for it. Entertaining in a home where you're comfortable will ease your nerves and radiate warmth. If your parents would rather host the party at a nearby restaurant, call as soon as possible and reserve your date. This is especially important if your engagement party falls near a major holiday.

If your engagement party is a less-than-formal affair, and you live in a part of the country where the weather is mild, take it to the outdoors. Have a picnic-type party. Have the bash in your backyard. Have the party in a nearby park. Having your party outside will allow you to invite more guests and cut down on decoration costs.

Do Serve Fun and Festive Food

The kind of food that you serve depends on several factors: formality of the event, time of day, season, available food budget, theme, and likes and dislikes of you and your fiancé. With that said, here are some ideas other than the traditional chicken and beef:

Serve Seasonal Veggies

Not only will they be easy to find, but also veggies are relatively inexpensive, quite yummy, and very healthy.

Go with a Themed Menu

If you're planning a medieval wedding, then start setting the mood early on. Serve medieval banquet foods such as smoked salmon with a honey mustard and fresh dill sauce and a cheese platter with a selection of breads.

Options for Hot Dishes

You can serve spicy Cajun beef, glazed honey ham, roast breast of turkey, swordfish, or shrimp.

Different Side Dishes

Why not offer stir-fried vegetables, herb-roasted potatoes, potato salad, pasta, or wild mushrooms?

Great Buffet Foods

Serve ham salad and tuna salad finger sandwiches, fried cheese, sausage balls, cheese puffs, Swedish meatballs and mini egg rolls, and other foods that are easy to eat with a minimum of cutlery.

Lively Presentations

You can make the same old boring beef and chicken quite exciting simply by presenting the food in a new and fun way. Your caterer should have some ideas to offer, so ask. Or, if you're throwing the party without the help of a caterer, use beautiful platters and decorative centerpieces with fresh foliage for a prettier presentation. If you're following a theme, let the theme guide your way. For instance, if it's a Texas barbecue, serve nachos in cowboy hats and place fresh flowers in cowboy boots. Have fun with your theme!

Provide Sparkling Juice for the Traditional Toast

Since the bride's parents host most engagement parties, it's a tradition for the father of the bride to give a toast to the happy couple. It's a way of formally announcing the engagement at the party. If your father is a little shy or if he is deceased, it's appropriate for any other close relative to offer a toast. Provide sparkling grape juice or cider for a nonalcoholic, yet tasty toast. And, make sure someone is on hand to record the entire party. You'll want that toast on tape.

Don't Feel Obligated to Have an Engagement Party

If an engagement party is absolutely out of the question due to timing or geographical challenges with your future husband, you have other options. Simply announce your news in your local newspapers.

Announcing Our Engagement: What's the Proper Way?

Q: What do I include in my engagement announcement?
A: The answer is usually dictated by the newspaper's specific style and restrictions, but here are a few guidelines and tips to assist you in crafting an awesome announcement.

- Always refer to the groom as the bridegroom because technically, a groom is someone who tends horses.
- If your parents are divorced, list both parents with their proper names. For example: "Mrs. Mika Brashears of Bedford, Indiana, and Mr. Robert Bridge of Fort Worth, Texas, announce the engagement of their daughter Breanna Bridge to . . ."

- If one of your parents is deceased, you might word your announce-ment like this: "Mrs. Janelle Lauder is pleased to announce the engagement of her daughter, Ginger Lauder, to Bernard Shaft. Miss Lauder is also the daughter of the late William Lauder."
- If both parents are deceased, a close relative or family friend can make the announcement, or you and your fiancé can make the announce-ment yourselves.
- Provide the newspaper with your full name, telephone numbers (both day and night), address, and the names and addresses of your parents. You should also include your education information (schools, col-leges, degrees attained, professional training), your occupation, and where you're currently employed.
- Be sure to include your fiancé's full name and address as well as his education and employment information.
- If you're still a student, it's perfectly okay to say, "Miss Bremmer will graduate from Indiana University with a bachelor's degree in jour-nalism in May 2005."

You may want to let your friends and relatives know about your excit-ing news by mailing them a simple, "Save the date," card. You can order these from any stationery store or wedding invitation catalogue. Or, you can cre-ate your own using your computer and laser printer. On this card, you might wish to word your message something like this: "Michelle Medlock and Jeffrey Adams are engaged to be married. Our special day would not be nearly as special without your presence. Please save the date—Saturday, August 31, 2004—and plan on joining us on our wedding day. For more information, please visit our Web site at www.wearesayingido.com online!"

Do Include Your Future Husband in the Planning

Yes, this is your time in life to shine. This is what you've always dreamed of. This is the time when it's all about you. But don't forget about your future husband. He may not want to take part in the party planning, but at least offer him that option. Let him know that his wishes and thoughts are important to you. This will not only set the tone for a successful party but also a successful marriage.

Do Enjoy Every Moment

In the hustle and bustle of planning for your big day, you need to keep telling yourself to enjoy the journey. Enjoy every minute of this special time in your life. From choosing the location of your engagement party to selecting the finger foods for the reception—bask in every moment. Don't let the weight of the details overwhelm you. Instead, look on every decision as a gift from God. You've already made the most important decision—you're about to marry the man of your dreams. This is exciting!

Ask one of your best friends to help you remember these precious moments by taking lots of pictures at every party. Then, even if all of this planning and partying seems like a blur by the time you say, "I do," you'll have pictures to help you remember every magical moment.

Don't Just Plan for the Party

Don't just plan for the engagement party—plan for your marriage. As you plan your engagement party and pick out your dress and choose your attendants, make sure that you and your fiancé take time out for God and for each other. There are many wonderful Bible studies for couples that you two could share together. But, most importantly, pray with one another and set the tone for your life together.

Long after the engagement party photos have faded and your wedding dress has yellowed, you'll still have each other and the special love you share for one another and the Lord. Now, that's something really worth celebrating.

Tokens of Love: Give Your Groom a Great Gift

You don't have to give your future husband an engagement gift, but it certainly would be a nice touch. Men act as if they don't like all of that "mushy stuff," but truth be known, they like it just as much as we do. So, what do you get the most special man in your life during this most special time in your lives?

Here are some inexpensive suggestions to help you give your husband-to-be tokens of your affection that will show him just how much you truly love him.

Give him love coupons to use during the engagement period. One foot massage. One long, romantic walk. One picnic in the park. Get creative with your love coupons. Write them on red and pink note cards; punch a hole in the corner of the cards; tie them together with a red ribbon; and wrap them beautifully.

Bake him heart-shaped cookies and deliver them to his doorstep on the night before the engagement party. Give him a kiss goodnight and tell him, "Tomorrow, we officially announce our plans to join our lives together for a lifetime, but just for the record—my heart has been yours for a long time."

Present your future husband with a shadow box filled with special mementos from your courtship: concert tickets, pressed flowers, pictures of times together, programs from special events, and so on.

Give him a gift basket filled with champagne glasses, a bottle of sparkling grape juice, Hershey Kisses®, a CD of love songs, and a book of romantic poetry. Use your imagination, and then wrap it in tulle, tying the top with a red-wired ribbon.

Present him with a journal full of memories—things you've written about him, thoughts you've had about him, qualities that attracted you to him, dreams you wish to fulfill together. He will enjoy reading flattering remarks, reminiscing about your relationship, and discovering how much you care for him.

Give your future husband a couple's devotional book. Inside, write him a special note saying, "I want us to grow closer to God as we grow closer together."

Use your head and your heart to find a great gift for your bridegroom. It's the perfect way to kick off your engagement and your life together.

MICHELLE MEDLOCK ADAMS is an award-winning writer and popular writers' conference speaker. Author of fifteen books, Michelle's latest releases include: *No Boys Allowed! Devotions for Girls* (Zonderkidz, 2004); *Sparrow's New Song* (Ideals Children's Books, 2004) and *Daily Wisdom for Working Women* (Barbour Publishing, 2004). Michelle married her high school sweetheart, Jeff, and they have two daughters. Visit her at www.michellemedlockadams.com.

17

CHAPTER

Wedding Celebrations

Rebeca DeBoard

EVERYTHING IN LIFE should be covered in prayer—and some things should be drowned in it. Planning a wedding is one of those events that will find you more often than not on your knees wailing pitifully before the throne. "Why can't they make that dress in size 14?" "Why are roses three times as expensive when they're starring in a wedding?" "What is the difference between butter cream and fondant?" "How do I tell Great-Aunt Edna that we're not following her suggestion of fuchsia bridesmaid dresses?" "Why is my groom so calm about all of this?"

Take a deep breath. Now, grab a pen and paper and write down these words: I am in love with an amazing man whom God has made just for me. Our wedding will be a day of celebrating this extraordinary gift. It will revolve around our love of each other and of Christ. I will not freak out.

Now go tape that to your bathroom mirror. Trust me, you're going to need it. A wedding can be one of two things in your life. It can be a day of relief, exhaustion, and headache. Or it can be a day of happiness, laughter, and love. Only you can make that decision.

As you're certainly becoming aware, many tasks must be completed to have a wonderful wedding. Let's step through seven major ones that relate to entertaining, and look at the details contained within each.

TASK ONE: Setting Your Priorities— Revealing Your Identities

Remember when you thought his antique car collection had absolutely no purpose in life? Or when you looked at all those Snowbabies you collected and thought—what do I do with these *now*? Well, look no further, dear bride, for you have found your answer. Taking a second look at your collections and interests will help you set the tone for the wedding. This day should be a reflection of your relationship, so splurge on wildflowers if that's what shows your personality. You have a wild and crazy groom? Put him in a purple tuxedo. Don't think about what everyone else will say about your wedding— the day isn't supposed to reflect their favorites.

How do you know what will accurately convey to your guests the uniqueness of you and your loved one? Try this. Plan a quiet dinner for two one night and take the following set of questions with you. Discuss them with your fiancé and see what sort of picture develops.

- What is your favorite musical instrument? What do you love about it? The shape of it? The sound it makes? The feelings it brings?
- What do you think is the single best thing you bring to the world or to our relationship?
- Where is your favorite place to hang out? (If the answer is in front of the television, then ask the following question instead.) Choose which

---

"... You have stolen my heart with one glance of your eyes ..." (Song of Sol. 4:9) of these you would rather hang out in for a few hours: (a) a smoky blues club with blue lights, low music, and a live singer with a throaty voice, (b) the symphony with violins, pianos, and harps where all the men are in tuxedos and the women are in long, sparkly dresses, (c) a tropical island with blazing sun, warm sand, suntan oil, and the sound of seagulls crying over crashing waves, or (d) a stone castle surrounded by lush green countryside with wrought iron light fixtures, marble floors, and bagpipes playing in the background?

- If we were planning this wedding with absolutely no thought for the preferences of anyone coming, what would you do?
- Have you ever thought about your wedding day? What did you see in your mind's eye? Describe it to me. What colors were there?

By the time you have obtained his thoughts on these questions, you will probably begin to get a sense of his style. Be sure to incorporate those things he loves into your wedding day. For instance, if he chose the stone castle, see if you can find a bagpipe player for the pre-wedding music. If he chose the island, perhaps you can have an island-themed reception complete with palm trees and leis!

TASK TWO: Sign Me Up!

You have probably already found the plethora of Web sites devoted to helping brides make their blissful dreams come true. If a wedding planner is not in your budget (which we'll discuss in a bit), these sites are your new best friends. Specifically, check out www.weddingchannel.com. You'll find everything you could ever ask for to help plan a wedding, including an itemized budget, guest list, reception, ideas, and more. Keeping all of these lists in one place, such as weddingchannel.com, is a true time-saver. Set aside an hour or so to search the Internet and go ahead and sign up for at least two, if not more, wedding site mailing lists. Soon, your inbox will be full of special deals and offers for everything from disposable wedding cameras to free tuxedos!

✒ TASK THREE: Budget

And speaking of free stuff, it's time to determine how much money you have to work with and where you need to concentrate those funds. This is not the time to take a nap. Budgets can actually be fun. Think of it as a puzzle. You have a certain amount of dollars to work with. Which position does each dollar fit into perfectly?

Be sure that you keep your groom's answers to the questions in Task One handy while formulating a budget. Whether you utilize an Internet budget template, make one of your own, or choose one from another source, try to make your expenditures reflect your personalities.

For instance, if your husband-to-be decided that a smoky blues club was his choice of a place to relax, then spending $3,000 on palm trees and leis for an island-themed reception is probably a bad idea. Perhaps you could hold your reception in a blues club? Or have your bridesmaids wear gowns reminiscent of the 1920s and '30s, when his favorite music was playing. Get creative. Your wedding can be *anything* you make it!

✒ TASK FOUR: Location, Location, Location

Now that you have your theme, it's time to find the location for your wedding. You will need to have this task completed at least four months before the wedding (six months or more is better). When deciding upon a wedding site, it is important to learn the church's restrictions and policies regarding decoration and time. Most churches now have a "wedding packet" that will alert you to any unusual policies or rules. Remember that your wedding does not have to be in a church—God is everywhere. You can make your vows in

---

"He has taken me to the banquet hall, and his banner over me is love."
(Song of Sol. 2:4)

an art museum, a botanical garden, beachside, or just about anywhere you can imagine.

Remember these things when picking a wedding site:

- How far is the wedding site from my reception site? How will guests get from one to the other?
- Will the number of guests I am inviting be able to comfortably fit into this space?
- Are the decorations that I have in mind a possibility at this site?
- Does this site reflect the personality and desires of both my groom and me?

As an alternative, you might want to consider going away to get married. If your guest list that was supposed to stay at 50 people has grown to 250, consider a "location" wedding. That does not preclude you from completing your vows in a church. Where is the oldest church of your denomination? For example, Frederick Evangelical Lutheran Church is located on the beautiful island of St. Thomas in the U.S. Virgin Islands. It is also the oldest Lutheran church in the Western Hemisphere. For someone who attends a Lutheran church but would like to have a location wedding, this is a perfect choice. Research the beginnings of your own denomination and see what pops up. You could also research the all-inclusive resorts, such as Sandals. Many such resorts can incorporate your wedding into your honeymoon trip for one fee. Check out www.sandals.com for more details.

TASK FIVE: Making Vendor Contacts

Wherever you decide to have your wedding and reception, you will need to make contact with vendors. Florists, caterers, photographers, videographers, musicians, and bakers are just a few of the experts you will probably call upon to make this day special. Remember that the vendor is working for *you*. You should not be pressured into purchasing anything you do not

> "Strengthen me with raisins, refresh me with apples, for I am faint with love." (Song of Sol. 2:5)

want or completing any activity in a manner you do not wish. Ask your friends and coworkers if they have recommendations. Check out the Internet. Some states have a Special Events Association or Wedding Coordinators Association. Call your local Chamber of Commerce and inquire about associations in your area.

Think for a bit on the theme of your reception. Continue to incorporate both the style of your groom that you learned about in Task One and your own style. Talk with your vendors so that they have a complete picture of the ideas and moods you want to convey at both the wedding and reception.

TASK SIX: Bliss!

To ensure that you can sit back and bask in the glow of love celebrated all day long during your wedding day, find someone who can be the contact for last-minute glitches. A cousin or one of the mothers is usually a great pick for this role. Give this person the authority to handle whatever might go wrong while you're getting your hair fixed or donning that perfect gown. This is your day. Enjoy it and embrace it. This day will be cherished for years to come.

TASK SEVEN: Finishing Touch

Upon your return from the honeymoon, be prepared to begin filling out thank-you cards for all of the lovely gifts and acts of service you received along the way. You might want to consult *Easy Etiquette* by Sharon Paskoff for samples of well-written thank-you notes. Or browse the shelves in your local bookstore to see what etiquette books are offered there. Whatever resource

> "His left arm is under my head, and his right arm embraces me." (Song of Sol. 2:6)

you utilize, try to get the cards out within a week. This first task as a married lady shouldn't be put off.

Now that you have read the primer on wedding preparation, you're probably wondering how on earth you will fit all of this activity into your busy life. Never fear, the time-saving list is here!

Wedding Lunch Hours

Use your lunch hour to take care of small tasks, make phone calls, or complete research on the Internet.

Wedding Weekends

Set aside five hours for two Saturdays per month before the wedding. This should give you plenty of time to meet with vendors and visit possible wedding/reception sites. It also ensures that you will also have time for the groom!

Organization

Repeat the mantra, "The list is my friend." Write down everything you need to accomplish or consult the to-do list provided at www.weddingchannel.com.

> "...That He who began a good work in you will carry it on to completion..." (Phil. 1:6)

Prayer

"Do not be anxious about anything, but in everything, by prayer and petition, with thanksgiving, present your requests to God. And the peace of God, which transcends all understanding, will guard your hearts and your minds in Christ Jesus" (Phil. 4:6, 7).

REBECA DeBOARD lives in Nashville, Tennessee, with her husband, Charles, and three basset hound mixes (Wilson, Cole, and Sophie). She is the publicist for WestBow Press, the fiction imprint of Thomas Nelson, Inc.

Rehearsal Dinners

DiAnn Mills

A MEMORABLE REHEARSAL dinner can be a snap, or it can be a nightmare. Decide right now that this undertaking will be fun and easy, and the result will be an affair you can remember with pride. This is a joyous celebration, the eve of your son's wedding. Tomorrow he begins a wonderful new life with his chosen bride and the fulfillment of many hopes and dreams. Tomorrow you welcome your new daughter with open arms and recognize your role as mother has moved to another realm.

For the bride and her family, the rehearsal dinner is one less worry in the unfolding of a fairy-tale wedding. This is the time for the bride and her parents to leave wedding stress behind, after the often-hectic events leading up to the rehearsal, and step into a comfortable and inviting atmosphere.

> "I delight greatly in the LORD; my soul rejoices in my God. For he has clothed me with garments of salvation and arrayed me in a robe of righteousness, as a bridegroom adorns his head like a priest, and as a bride adorns herself with her jewels." (Isa. 61:10)

When our son was married, we decided the goal of the rehearsal dinner was to demonstrate the honor and pride felt for all those involved in the ceremony as well as the love for our son. I admit to being a sentimental mom who shed a lot of tears as I thought about the change in my son's life.

Many times, the rehearsal dinner is the groom's parents' single opportunity to shine, not in the amount of money spent on a gala event, but in the time taken to ensure the wedding party enjoys the evening. If you display a poor attitude and believe the preparations are a burden, no one will enjoy the time of blessing and fellowship.

If your knees are knocking and your pulse is racing at the mere mention of a planned and organized rehearsal dinner, relax. The step-by-step process listed in this chapter will help. Believe me; this can be easy.

Whether the groom desires a family barbecue for the wedding rehearsal dinner or a sit-down dinner at an exclusive restaurant, proper planning sets the stage for a memorable occasion. Since the atmosphere reflects the groom's personal taste, enlist his ideas and give careful consideration to those things that are important to him.

Since many times it is the groom's responsibility to coordinate the events for the men in the wedding party, I suggest sending a letter to all of the groomsmen and ushers that contains the following information:

- A "thank you" for agreeing to participate in your son's wedding celebration and an acknowledgment of how much you appreciate their friendship and support.
- A complete schedule of what is happening the weekend of the wedding from the time they pick up their tuxes to the time they must be returned.

"Do not forget to entertain strangers, for by so doing some people have entertained angels without knowing." (Heb. 13:2)

Have extra copies of the letter available for guys who have a tendency to misplace things. This ensures that the groom and his men have no excuse to be late for any of the events. The bride and her parents also might appreciate a copy.

The Planning Stages

The information that follows is designed to help you dance your way through the rehearsal dinner. Highlight the portions you need to incorporate into your plans, and grab a notepad to jot down those things that waltz around your mind. Don't forget your dancing shoes!

Establish a Budget

As much as you want the finest rehearsal dinner in the country, monetary considerations should come first. Make sure you have discussed the budget with your spouse and in some cases the groom. Utilizing the most exquisite restaurant where the hungry crowd is served a small amount of appetizers and water is not only inappropriate but invites criticism.

God calls us to be good stewards, and emerging yourself in debt to pay for a rehearsal dinner doesn't fall under sound money management. Financial responsibility and adhering to an established budget also models excellent standards for your son's future monetary decisions and goals.

The Guest List

The next item to tackle is who will attend the dinner. Traditionally, the wedding party—which includes the bridesmaids, ring bearer, flower girl, groomsmen, and ushers with their guests—is at the top of the list. Add the minister, organist, soloists, wedding coordinator, grandparents, great grandparents, photographer, and all the others who play a role in the wedding and reception—and their guests. You also can extend an invitation to family and friends who

> Before you ask for the guest list, consider menu options, take a peek into your savings account, or ask God for guidance and wisdom. After all, God wants the best for all those in attendance just like you do.

have traveled from out of town, but this is not a requirement. Ask the bride for the addresses from the wedding invitation list to assist in mailing the rehearsal dinner invitations to your guests.

When you're listing the guests, don't forget the bride, groom, and yourself. The list can contain as many guests as you deem necessary or the budget allows. Invitations can be as simple as those created on your computer to elegant, embossed stationery that match the wedding invitations. The following is an example of what to include:

Type of Event: Rehearsal Dinner
Honoring: Bride and Groom
Date:
Time:
Place: List the complete address of the dinner site
Given by:
RSVP Deadline with phone number

If possible, I suggest including a map showing a route from the rehearsal location to where the dinner will be served along with written directions. This can be an envelope insert. For your records, keep a spreadsheet listing each invited guest, children if any, their address, phone number, and the date the guest responded to the RSVP. It's helpful to have this printed out and close to the phone.

Dinner Location and Menu

What everyone will eat is important. I remember many elegant functions where the food was tasteless, overcooked, and a small token of what the evening represented. I decided this wouldn't happen to me. Many fine rehearsal dinners take place in a church's fellowship facility or in a private home; others are held in a country club or restaurant. The setting is limited only by your imagination. Ask those who have hosted rehearsal dinners for their input and recommendations.

The most time-efficient manner of finding a location is to search online. Web sites often have pictures of the grounds and banquet rooms. Make note of how many guests the facility can accommodate. Menu choices and options and costs should be posted as well. Do you want an appetizer? Do you want an elegant or simple dessert? Perhaps live music is important to you, or perhaps the dinner will include a number of children. Always ask. I found that the banquet coordinator is often willing to do far more than advertised. Giving guests a selection of food and beverage is recommended—at least two choices. Will you have a salad bar, or do you want the guests served? Alcohol is expensive and religious preference may eliminate that consideration.

Your budget will help you select the type of dinner and menu. Be sure to make an appointment to view the banquet facilities. Plan the visits early on, and reserve the chosen facility as far in advance as possible. A deposit, usually nonrefundable, is required. Do not hesitate to phone the facility with any questions.

Seating is vital to the success of the dinner. Make a diagram of the room or rooms that you plan to use, and arrange tables with the immediate wedding party as the focal point. To simplify matters, give the banquet coordinator a copy of the diagram. Eliminate any confusion or strife that plagues even the best of families, and use place cards for the guests. The bride and groom may want to be consulted on this.

Personalizing the Evening

Does the host facility supply table decorations? If not, consider renting the needed items. Of course, if you have five other sons who will one day require a rehearsal dinner, then your best option may be to purchase some of the things.

I suggest providing a small gift at each place setting in memory of the occasion. One of our sons was married a week before Christmas. I found Christmas mugs, filled them with Hershey Hugs® and Hershey Kisses® then attached a ribbon and note that read: "Hugs and Kisses for the Mr. and Mrs." Place at least one portable camera at each table for the guests to snap pictures of what is happening around them. You can collect these at the close of the evening. Even if you decide to hire a professional photographer for the rehearsal dinner, the impromptu shots from the guests will be valuable to the bride and groom.

Your rehearsal dinner also could include a printed program. This can help everyone know what is to happen and when. Or, jotting down a note might be sufficient. I was such a basket case that I needed reminders. Don't forget to have someone ask the blessing for the food and for the evening.

Since the wedding is the following day—and you do want the wedding party to get a good night's sleep—keep the evening short and stick to the time restraints provided by the facility. Here are a few examples of what activities often accommodate a rehearsal dinner after everyone has eaten:

- Members of the wedding party can give a brief testimony of their friendship to the bride or groom, including humorous or serious accountings.
- Bridesmaids' and groomsmen's gifts can be distributed.
- The parents of the bride and groom may want to say something to their child or the wedding party.
- The parents of the groom may want to give the bride and groom a gift, which could be humorous.
- The mother of the groom may want to have an "apron-cutting" ceremony. I gave my son a gift of an old apron, one he used in his younger days when we cooked or baked. With the apron was a pair of scissors. I tied the apron around his waist and told him that as of the next day he belonged to his wife and not his mommy. I cut the strings and handed them to his bride.
- A letter of release to the son from his parents.

The following is an example of the letter that my husband read at the rehearsal dinner. It is based on the book *Tender Warrior* by Stu Weber.

"Like arrows in the hand of a warrior, so are the children of one's youth. How blessed is the man whose quiver is full of them."

To _____ ,

To a world very much needing his character, his gifts, his skill, and his love for Christ, we do proudly and humbly announce in the manner of our heavenly Father, this is our beloved son _____, in whom we are well pleased. Like an arrow fashioned not to remain in the quiver, but to be released into the heart of its target, we release _____ to adulthood. We know him to be thoughtful, capable, and mature. He is the message we release to a world we will never see. He is a man. We release him to his manhood and all of its responsibilities. To the cherishing of his godly and supportive wife _____, to the beginning and raising by God's grace and design of believing children. And to the commission of the Lord Jesus Christ Himself to go into all the world, making followers of all people, teaching them to observe the rich and life-giving truths of His holy Scriptures.

_____, we love you, we're extremely proud of you, and we release you to the target of being all you can be in Christ. Continue to exemplify the ideal of placing God first, others second, and yourself third. You will always be our son. You will never again be our little boy. Thank you, _____, for having graced our lives with your remarkable sonship. You have blessed us richly.

Your very fulfilled parents,

There weren't many dry eyes after that reading, including my husband and son.

> When I stand before God at the end of my life, I would hope that I would not have a single bit of talent left and could say, "I used everything you gave me." —ERMA BOMBECK

Winding Up

Thank all for attending the dinner and dismiss your guests. Remind them to take their gifts in memory of the evening. Make sure you remain until all of the guests have left. Take care of the financial responsibilities and/or any cleanup if necessary.

Now that you see how simple planning a wedding rehearsal dinner is, are you ready to dance?

DIANN MILLS is author of several novels and novellas, as well as nonfiction, short stories, articles, and devotions. She has contributed to several nonfiction compilations. She is a favorite author of Heartsong Presents' readers. She is a founding board member for American Christian Romance Writers and a member of Inspirational Writers Alive. DiAnn and her husband reside in Houston, Texas. Visit her at www.diannmills.com.

19

CHAPTER

Anniversary Celebrations

BEVERLY HENRY

THE CANDLES are lit, the fragrance of favorite foods fills the air, and soft music plays in the background. You place a rose across his plate and prop a card against his glass. You're eager with anticipation to hear his car in the driveway, wondering what little surprises he'll have for you. You know he's just as excited as you to celebrate this special night. It's your first anniversary. Nothing can equal the romance that accompanies that first remembrance of your wedding day.

But as the years progress, will the romance be gone from the remembrance? Will the memory become mundane? What kind of things can you expect on the fifth, twelfth, and, even that milestone, your twenty-fifth anniversary? Are there ways to keep the excitement, the freshness, and the loveliness of that day alive? The answer is yes. But as with any aspect of your marriage, it takes time, thought, preparation, and an adventuresome spirit to

"The mandrakes send out their fragrance, and at our door is every delicacy, both new and old, that I have stored up for you, my lover." (Song of Sol. 7:13)

keep the embers glowing and ready to ignite into the fires of romance. Before you roast marshmallows over those romantic flames, some practical planning needs to take place. Let's take a look at some important and necessary steps to successful anniversary celebrations.

Budget

Your budget should be the first thing to consider when planning your anniversary. This isn't just about how much money you have to spend. Your time, resources, and talents all have a bearing in what it will cost. Remember that you can make a memorable evening regardless of how elegant or elemental your plans.

When you're short on funds, get creative. College or high school plays, as well as cultural, community, or seasonal events, can be a lot of fun. Ethnic festivals, sporting events, antique shows, or craft fairs might provide the right atmosphere. Visit your own town as a tourist; spend a night at a bed-and-breakfast and go sightseeing. Our town offers an historical walking tour that tells the story of local buildings, plus an observatory and museum of excellent quality—great places to create a romantic day away. You can incorporate these events into your anniversary celebration by adding a picnic lunch or enjoying specialty or regional foods. Sometimes sharing an ice cream cone in your favorite outdoor spot or going for a long, quiet walk can be just the respite from a hectic routine that you both need for spiritual refreshment and reconnection.

My husband and I once took a picnic dinner to a local resort and ate by a small lake, complete with entertainment provided by a mama duck and her ducklings. We called ahead and got permission from the resort—don't just assume it's allowed. I packed the good dishes and even put in crystal glassware

"Suppose one of you wants to build a tower. Will he not first sit down and estimate the cost to see if he has enough money to complete it?" (Luke 14:28)

and a candle for us to light. After dinner we walked the grounds of the resort by moonlight. Some of our more memorable anniversaries were ones where we didn't spend large amounts of money on dinners, entertainment, or gifts but gave each other the priceless gift of our time and attention.

A simple meal is always a winner. Fix your favorite homemade soup, warm bread, and a crisp salad for your next intimate anniversary dinner. Finish with an elegant English trifle or homemade cream puffs and elegant coffee.

ENGLISH FRUIT TRIFLE (NO BAKE)

Pound Cake—cut into bite-size pieces
1 package French Vanilla Instant Pudding Mix
1³/₄ cups milk

8 oz. container Cool Whip
2 packages frozen berries (Strawberries, Raspberries or Blackberries), thawed

Mix pudding and milk according to package directions and then fold in Cool Whip. Arrange some of the cake pieces in bottom of a clear glass bowl. Spoon a layer of mixed berries (with juice) over cake, add a layer of the pudding mixture, repeat, ending with pudding. Add a few berries to the top as decoration. Refrigerate till well chilled and serve in dessert cups.

CREAM PUFF DELIGHTS

¹/₂ cup water
¹/₄ cup butter

¹/₂ cup all purpose flour
2 eggs

Heat oven to 400 degrees. Heat water and butter to rolling boil in saucepan. Add flour, stirring vigorously over low heat until mixture

(Continued)

forms a ball (about 1 minute). Beat in eggs, all at once and continue beating till mixture is smooth. Drop by ¼ cupfuls onto ungreased cookie sheet. Bake until puffed and golden (30-40 minutes). Cool thoroughly.

Slice off tops and scoop out doughy insides, leaving a crisp shell. Fill with your favorite ice cream flavor, add top of puff and finish with a drizzle of hot fudge sauce.

ELEGANT PARTY COFFEE

Prior to brewing, add ½ teaspoon pure vanilla extract to the carafe of your coffeemaker and sprinkle 1 teaspoon nutmeg over the coffee grounds. Brew as usual for a rich flavorful cup of coffee.

Tip: To help keep coffee hot, add liquid creamer to the cup prior to pouring in the coffee.

On those occasions when you do have extra funds with which to splurge, be adventuresome and bold. Seek out a restaurant you've never tried before. Visiting a Thai or Greek restaurant can become an adventure that opens up new vistas. If you find you really don't like the food, you have at least created a fun memory. Do something you've never done before. Celebrate with an anniversary breakfast, visit a working farm or ranch, take a flying lesson, or go on a whitewater rafting trip or a hot-air balloon ride. You will set the tone for whatever you decide to do by your enthusiasm and joy of the adventure.

Gifts

Just as a wedding ring is an outward sign of an inward commitment, so are gifts that you give to one another on your anniversary. A gift is a visible, tangible way to commemorate your vows and say, "I love you, and I'd marry you all over again." How to observe this part of your celebration may vary from year to year and couple to couple. One couple might decide early on to only

> "Every good and perfect gift is from above, coming down from the Father of the heavenly lights, who does not change like shifting shadows." (James 1:17)

buy a gift they can both enjoy, like furniture, fine art, or home accessories. Another couple may choose to surprise each other with romantic items they know the other would enjoy—jewelry or a hand-carved chess set. And yet another couple may set a very small price limit, ensuring creativity and some interesting surprises.

No matter what you decide about gifts, a card is a must. Lots of us have a hard time expressing our thoughts with words, but there are people who do this for a living. Make use of their talent and buy a card that expresses what is in your heart. If you're the creative type, and know just what you want to say, get out your paper, scissors, glue, and imagination and make a memory. Heartfelt, homemade cards carry a message of love and tenderness you cannot buy. Either way, homemade or store-bought, a card is a wonderful gift. I've kept every card my husband has ever given me, and occasionally, I get them out and read all the wonderful things he's said to me over the years.

Take some time to reflect on what makes your spouse happy, what gives them joy and makes them feel loved. This may bring you new insight on how to celebrate with gifts for your next anniversary. Remember, the best gift you can give is your heart.

Parties

Parties are as much fun to give as to receive. A party is a great way to celebrate a milestone anniversary like a tenth, twenty-fifth, or fiftieth, or to commemorate a year that holds a special event such as the birth of a child or renewal of your marriage vows. Parties can vary from a formal, elegant, or catered affair to a backyard barbecue with kids, family, and friends. Decide if you want a theme, and then capitalize on that. If your anniversary is in the

---

LOVE LETTERS

Choose some beautiful stationery and write a love letter to your spouse. Thank God for them and list the gifts they bring to your marriage, like faithfulness, diligence, and a gentle heart. Include Scripture that describes their character or Christlike qualities.

"I thank God . . . as night and day I constantly remember you in my prayers" (2 Tim. 1:3).

---

summer, a Hawaiian luau or beach party would be fun, or, if you were married in fall, a hayride might be the place to start. Brainstorm to see what is of interest to you and your spouse. If golf is your passion, use that as your base and come up with theme-related invitations, decorations, and food. "The Seventh Annual Jim and Margie Pro-Marriage Tour" could use tin cups as party favors filled with treats, games of Tiddly Winks throughout the room to encourage guest competition, and food arranged on a "green" with flags identifying the different food dishes and foil-wrapped chocolate golf balls. Your love of vintage autos might spark the "Twelfth Anniversary Thompson Car Rally." Involve your family or friends in a road trip around your area and stop at scenic points of interest for different courses of a picnic dinner. The sky's the limit!

A few years ago we hosted a tenth anniversary party for some friends. They had originally married with no family or friends present. Although they wanted to renew their vows in a ceremony, they wanted a small, intimate atmosphere. Using tones of cream, gold, and white, we transformed our open living room/dining area into a small chapel and reception hall. We dug out the Christmas white twinkle lights and strung them all around the room at ceiling level. Furniture was moved out of the room, and chairs were set up for the guests. Draping wide cream-colored satin ribbon from row to row, and adding fresh flower bouquets to the chairs at the end of each row created a center aisle. An altar at one end of the room with a podium for the

"He has taken me to the banquet hall, and his banner over me is love."
(Song of Sol. 2:4)

pastor was flanked by small candelabras. In the dining area, we set up a table with white linen for the buffet dinner and a round card table for the cake. We purchased a white-on-white store-bought two-layer cake and adorned it with strings of miniature pearls and fresh white roses to create more of a wedding look. Cream-colored and gold candles were lit all around the room creating a soft glow complemented by the small white ceiling lights. We used soft, instrumental recorded music and the ambiance was one of quiet elegance—just what the bride wanted. It was a memorable evening complete with photos, cake cutting, and toasts to the couple by each guest. It was also a wonderful experience for their young children to see their parents renewing their marriage vows.

Whatever way you choose to commemorate your wedding anniversary will be unique to you and your spouse. These celebrations will create a continuum of memories that you will relive in years to come. Life inevitably brings change with each passing year and your anniversary is a wonderful time to reflect on those changes, reminisce about the past and look with hope and expectancy to the love and future you share.

BEVERLY HENRY is active in the creative arts department of her church, directing, writing, and acting. She speaks to various women's groups and is currently working on a devotional book about pastor's wives. Beverly resides in Flagstaff, Arizona.

Baby Showers

PATTI SHADBOLT

THE BIRTH of every child is a gift from heaven. A baby shower, given by loving friends and relatives, is a perfect way to celebrate that special gift from God to the family. You'll remember forever the shared prayer, excitement, and rejoicing that comes with a shower.

Some types of baby showers work best before the birth, some after, and a few in either instance. Here, you'll find ideas for games, devotions, and gifts to make each kind of shower successful. By adding your own personal touches, you will be able to create a baby shower that the new mother will fondly remember for years to come.

Themed Baby Showers

Proverbs 15:13 tells us, "A happy heart makes the face cheerful." Themed baby showers do just that. They incite smiles, kindle giggles, and build loving memories, no matter whether it's the mother's first baby or her fourth or more.

A baby is God's opinion that life should go on. —CARL SANDBURG

Scrapbook Themed Shower

With scrapbooking so popular these days, why not have the shower at a local scrapbook store? Or, gather in your home and provide scrapbook materials. Everyone can take part in preparing pages for the baby's homecoming, first bath, baptism or dedication ceremony, first steps, first tooth, first birthday, first baby food, first Christmas (or other holidays), and so on. The parents can add pictures later as the events take place. The resulting scrapbook will be treasured for years to come.

Couples Shower

Consider assigning each couple a particular type of gift around a theme. Ideas might include sick baby items, bath time items, play time items, baby's first meal items, teething needs, bedtime items, needs for baby's first outing, emergency needs, Grandma's bag for baby's visits, and so on. Again, it is the memories of the evening and the time together with couples that are most important. After all, when a friend gives a present, it is not the present, but the friend that is the gift.

GAME IDEAS

Give each daddy attending a "taste test" of popular prepared jarred baby foods. You might just find out who is the greatest "spitting image."

Consider asking the father-to-be to answer a list of baby questions ahead of time. Ideas might include: Who will give Junior his first bath? What will be Daddy and baby's first outing together? Will Dad wish to cut the cord if asked? Who will be the first person the mother will call after baby is born? Then see if the mother comes up with the same answers at the shower. This game is sure to spark conversation and reminiscences.

> A man finds out what is meant by a spitting image when he tries to feed cereal to his infant. —IMOGENE FEY

A third game that is sure to spur a smile from even the most difficult face to crack requires a little preplanning. Ask each guest to bring his or her own baby photo. Couples are then given the opportunity to guess the identity of each picture. This is a game where fingers are pointed and chuckles stifled.

In lieu of devotions for the couple's baby shower, pretty note cards can be provided for "Advice for Fathers from Fathers." Males often give advice we females forget to take into consideration. For example, "Place baby strapped in their car seat on top of the running clothes dryer if baby cries while Mommy is away from home." This is as close to the simulation of driving as you can get!

Diaper or Formula Shower

A diaper or a formula shower will be appreciated for months after the new baby arrives. For a diaper shower, guests can bring a package of any size or brand of disposable diapers. It's the same idea for a formula shower. Be sure you find out from the mother in advance whether she plans to use a service or disposable diapers and if she plans to breast-feed or feed the baby formula. See if she's settled on a brand based on her doctor's recommendation.

Or, buy a diaper bag before the shower, and have each guest contribute to filling it with items such as a thermometer, diaper wipes, cold medicines, gas drops, small toys, pacifiers, baby pain reliever, and so on.

Second/Third Child Showers

"Seasoned" mothers often do not need the basics for their new baby, but appreciate gathering with friends. The gifts can be substantially less crucial. Consider calling this a "Sprinkle" rather than a shower on the invitation.

These are smaller, more informal gatherings. Guests may decide on a group gift of something the mother specifically requests rather than individual smaller items. If the sex of this baby is different from older siblings, newborn clothing in either blue or pink would be appreciated.

Another thoughtful, less costly gift is a homemade IOU Coupon Book. Each guest attending decides in advance what service she can provide for the growing family. Examples include free babysitting, laundry assistance, a "parents-only" night out, admission tickets to a children's museum for a family outing, or coupons for pizza or movies.

Bed-rest Mother's Shower

Friends share not only cups of laughter, but also cups of sorrow. For many reasons, a woman today may find herself confined to bed rest for part of her pregnancy. It is in this time that we need to plan a shower that may well be titled "Friends in Deed."

One of the difficult things about prescribed bed rest is that the dust bunnies lurking under your bed and in the corners appear so much larger to your eyes than anyone else's. It might be especially helpful to this mother to plan a baby shower with friends who will come clean her house, share a light lunch, and add laughter and frozen meals for future use. Small gifts such as playing cards, stationery, inspirational books, thank-you notes, and other items she can use even in bed would be appreciated.

Another idea for a bed rest shower might include pampering the woman with a pedicure, leg shaving, or professional massage.

Formal Baby Shower

This type of shower is usually catered and decorations are extravagant. The hostess might consider a menu with all "baby foods." The first course could include salad made with baby spring greens, baby carrots, baby corn, baby asparagus, mandarin oranges, cooked cubed chicken, toasted almonds, and poppy seed dressing. The second course could be made up of mini-quiches and bite-size muffins. Fruit tarts, small finger delicacies, and chocolate-dipped fruits could round out the meal, and available drinks could include coffee or tea in demitasse cups or sparkling cider in champagne glasses with a small blueberry (for baby boys) or raspberry (for baby girls) floating in the bottom.

Decorations

The decorations are the little extras that will make your baby shower memorable. Using disposable paper plates, napkins, and cups in blue or pink will add to the "look," as well as to the ease of preparation and cleanup for a casual event.

A great gift that also doubles as a decoration is a diaper cake. Roll up seventy-two small disposable diapers and tie them with a ribbon. Each of the diapers is stacked to resemble a layer cake, with each layer tied with ribbon colored appropriately for the sex of the baby. If the baby shower is given before the birth and the sex is still unknown, blue and pink ribbons can be alternated. The diaper cake is decorated with pacifiers, booties, toys, and so forth. The result is both attractive and useful.

An idea for a table centerpiece is a "rose bouquet" made from frilly little girl socks. The frill and lace along the top of the sock is gathered tightly with a running stitch and attached to heavy wire with florist tape. Artificial rose leaves are attached, making each flower a single stem "rose." The running stitch can easily be snipped, providing the new mother with several pairs of socks for newborns.

If you have sufficient time and want to make individual favors for each guest, a "pacifier" can be made from two white Life Savers® and a small yellow jellybean. The first Life Saver® is laid flat with the jellybean forced through the hole on the upper side. (That becomes the nipple of the pacifier). The second Life Saver® is attached with a small bit of frosting glue (purchased or homemade) in an upright position to become the handle of the pacifier. These are really cute and go together quickly.

Gift Ideas

The best gift a friend can give is her presence, but a unique gift can serve as tangible evidence of our love.

The Magic Hanky

The Magic Hanky is one of the most unusual small gifts I have seen. Although the author is unknown, this little poem explains its use:

> I'm just a little hanky
> As you can plainly see.
> But with a few stitches,
> They made a bonnet out of me.
> I'll be worn home from the hospital
> Or on my baptism day.
> Then I'll be neatly pressed
> And carefully packed away.
> For on that wedding day
> Or so I have been told,
> Every well-dressed bride
> Must wear that something old.
> So what could be better
> Than to find little me;
> A few stitches snipped
> And a wedding hanky I'll be.
> And if perchance it is a boy,
> Someday he'll surely wed.
> What a special present for his bride,
> This hanky, once worn upon his head.

The hanky can be purchased or easily made. The directions to make it are so simple that they sound difficult. In actuality, the most difficult thing is finding an inexpensive, all-white hanky.

MAKING YOUR OWN MAGIC HANKY

First, you will need a hemstitched 10 in. x 10 in. handkerchief, preferably white. Tat an edging directly onto the hanky. Lay hanky on a flat surface and fold one end back about a half inch, and press the fold through a cloth. Then fold the opposite edge back about two and a half inches, then fold that edge back one inch. The result is a small accordion fold. Press this through a cloth as well.

Next, take a needle and white thread, and with a very long basting stitch, sew your thread through the half-inch fold that you made originally. Gather the fabric tightly, and tie the threads together in a knot. This makes it easy for someone to snip the thread later. Secure ribbon ties with a quick "X" stitch. Be sure and leave a long enough thread after you knot it so that the baby's mom can find it later.

Time Capsules

Shower guests can contribute to a "Mini-Time Capsule in a Diaper Pail" to be opened when baby turns eighteen or leaves home. Items that might be included are a newspaper from the baby's birth date, pictures of Mommy pregnant, party favors from the shower, prices of popular foods, titles of the latest movies, names of popular sports figures, letters of advice from the baby's grandparents, and so on. The diaper pail is glued shut after all the guests have placed their items inside.

Devotions

Devotions are an important part of the baby shower experience. Spiritual thoughts shared with friends and family set precedence for the new parents to continue a legacy of godly living.

As we partner with God in raising our children, we can also partner with friends in prayer for the child. The hostess of the baby shower can purchase pretty note cards and have the new mother list prayer requests she might have for her baby, for her expanding family, for her husband as father, and so forth. She will share those prayer requests with the guests. Each guest who wishes to be included will promise the new mother she will pray the requests for a determined time period; usually a month or so. This activity helps to bind friends together and forms even stronger friendships.

There will be many nights spent tending a sleepless newborn or ailing older child. Rather than fret over insufficient sleep, an older woman advised me to pray through the alphabet of "who I perceived God to be to me as a new mother" as I rocked my premature baby through so many restless nights. It is advice I now give many new mothers and can be used as a devotion during the shower. For example:

A—You are able to meet my needs.
B—You are my burden bearer.
C—Comfort my baby as I rock her.

Conclusion

A baby shower is a wonderful way to celebrate friendship and family, to enjoy laughter, and to recognize that times spent together make good memories. The best baby showers are simple. New mothers or mothers-to-be are usually tired and pulled in many directions. A "successful" baby shower need not be expensive or exhaustive to be fun for either the new parent or the hostess. An unknown person once commented that sharing a piece of bread with a friend could be a feast. As godly businesswomen and busy mothers, let's enjoy the feast of one another's company through successful simplicity.

PATTI SHADBOLT is a humorous motivational speaker and interactive Bible teacher whose passion includes Women's Ministry and Prayer Journaling. Patti's message to audiences is to seek God through prayer and make a conscious choice to find joy in every day, regardless of circumstance. She may be contacted through her Web site: www.pattishadbolt.com.

Retirement Parties

YVETTE THOMAS

THEY SELDOM give out gold watches when you retire these days. All the more reason, then, to honor our colleagues when they are ready to retire after years on the job. After all, some women spend more waking hours with their coworkers than with anyone else. Let's honor their dedication.

Let's say a colleague is saying "good-bye" after twenty, or even thirty, long years of work for a company that has been her home away from home. Loyalty and integrity have been her driving force and now it's time to celebrate these attributes about her. You would like to throw a creative retirement party that reflects her personality.

Dressing for Success

There are three important accessories that will help dress up the party:

Color

Who says that a retirement party has to be dull and boring? No way! Let's make it as splashy as possible. Use a dynamic, eye-catching color combination.

> Loyalty and integrity have been her driving force and now it's time to celebrate these attributes about her.

After all, color is an inexpensive way to decorate. The best way to begin is to find out the retiree's favorite colors. Begin building around her likes. If you're unable to find this out, here are several suggestions: purple and red, silver and blue, or gold and white.

Smell

Make sure that you have aromatic room scents to spray in the room minutes before guests arrive. The White Candle Barn Co. has two of my favorites: Watermelon (which would be perfect for a spring or summer occasion) or Tender Orchids (which gives the hint that you've decorated the entire room with fresh flowers). What woman doesn't like fresh flowers? This works well, even if you give your party at work in a cubicle!

Music

Have soft instrumental music playing in the background. Not too loud, not too soft, just enough to create a cozy feeling. Make sure it's instrumental so the music and guest won't be competing for attention. This light background music can be very conducive to enjoyable conversation.

Creating Successful Memories

Remember, this party is about celebrating her. Her accomplishments, rewards, and most of all her personality. If you know that she likes ice cream, have a few homemade ice cream churns available with fresh ice cream. If you know she enjoys an afternoon cappuccino, then by all means, try to borrow or rent a cappuccino machine in her honor. What a nice personal touch that says, "This is for you."

You will want to remember to "dress the party" with the right balance of celebrating her and giving her precious memories. Below are some inexpensive ideas that give a unique flavor to any retirement party.

Roast

Choose four or five people who have worked very closely with the honoree to get together and discuss her work at your company. They know her personality, quirks, likes and dislikes, habits, and so on. Have them sit at a six-foot table with all of the chairs facing her. Give each person three minutes to share his or her thoughts and cherished memories of the guest of honor. It could go something like this:

- I enjoyed working with her because she was always so gracious and kind.
- I enjoyed working with her because she was always on time and set a standard of excellence for our company.
- I enjoyed working with her because she made work fun. She always brought her smile with her to work!
- I enjoyed working with her because she knew how to turn bad situations into something positive!

Skit

Choose three or four people to act out a typical work scenario. You know what I'm talking about. Every office has situations that keep happening over and over. Deliberately make this a fun time. Use your imagination.

Words of Blessings

Have everyone in the room spontaneously take turns sharing how they feel about her, in their own words. Words of affirmation will go a long way.

Popcorn Prayer

Have the group assemble around her and then, just like popcorn, begin to pray. Pop—here is a prayer. Pop—someone else says a prayer. And whoever is holding the popcorn bag can be the one to conclude this time of the party. This is a nice way to spend time praying for her next venture or the next chapter in her life—and an appropriate time to thank God for all of the guest of honor's wonderful attributes.

Special Scriptures

Since this is a retirement party, you can bless her with Bible verses written within a "work" context and then explain the meaning of each verse after you've read it.

- "The laborer's appetite works for him; his hunger drives him on" (Prov. 16:26). After you finish reading the verse, say, "God gave you an unquenchable passion for your work here; it was obvious to all who were around you. You are a fine example for us to follow!"
- "The plans of the diligent lead to profit as surely as haste leads to poverty" (Prov. 21:5). After you finish reading the verse, say, "You have been an asset to our company. We have not only profited monetarily because of you, but we've also profited spiritually by your outstanding witness for the Lord."
- "My heart took delight in all my work, and this was the reward for all my labor" (Eccles. 2:10). After you finish reading the verse, say, "It was obvious that you enjoyed your work. You always gave 110 percent."
- "He will not forget your work and the love you have shown him as you have helped his people and continue to help them" (Heb. 6:10). After you finish reading, say, "God must be smiling in heaven today because of all of the love that you've shown us. As you have served us, you have served Him."

- Jesus said, "Well done, good and faithful servant . . ." (Matt. 25:21). After you finish reading the verse, say, "May God in heaven bless you for your faithfulness to our company and to us. It was an honor to work with you."

Helium Balloons

These can have a twofold purpose:

- Use them as decorations: To save money, ask around the office if someone has a helium tank you can borrow. If not, they cost around twenty dollars at your local party store.
- Use them as farewell favors: At the close of the event, divide the helium balloons up among the guests and go outside. Have everyone get in a circle, and one at a time, take turns sharing something significant about her and why you'll miss her, then let one balloon go. Take turns going around the circle until all of the balloons are gone.

INEXPENSIVE TIPS FOR DECORATING

- *Glitter:* Dust the table with a coordinating color.
- *Tissue Paper:* Find a beautiful coordinating pattern and use as a base for your centerpiece.
- *Gift Bags:* Any of those stores that sell items for a dollar or less will have a variety of gift bags you can fill with tissue paper to make inexpensive, attractive centerpieces.
- *Terracotta Pots:* Use them to hold silverware, napkins, or even ice if you line the pot with a garbage bag. (I've used a huge one to hold baked potatoes for a baked potato bar at a garden retirement party.)
- *Candles:* Small votive candles give a friendly ambiance to any room.

There is something very sweet about watching all of the balloons drift up to the heavens.

Memories to Keep

There are several things you can plan in advance that will make your retirement party extremely memorable. Here are some simple ideas that will give the party a very personal touch that she'll never forget.

Video

Ask someone to shoot video footage of everyone in the office saying his or her heartfelt good-byes. Don't rush through this; it could be one of the greatest treasures she'll enjoy in the coming days, months, and even years ahead. Start on the video at least one month in advance. If shown during the party, this could very well be one of the biggest highlights!

Favorite Song

Have someone type the words to her favorite song and distribute them to everyone to sing along at the party. Almost all songs are available on karaoke CDs. How cute would this be as a finale?

Handwritten Notes

Give everyone at least two weeks to create his or her own handwritten notes. Length doesn't matter; it's the thought that counts. Purchase a nice photo album and place each separate note onto a page of the photo album. This will be a treasured memento.

Pictures

Have your resident photographer take candid shots around the office. Have everyone assemble around her desk while she's out to lunch.

Disposable Cameras

Place these in various locations around the party and instruct people to take random pictures. Attach a small note to each camera with specific directions that say, "Please help us create memories by taking a picture." At the end of the party, give the cameras to her as part of your farewell gift.

The Perfect Gift

My best ideas have always come from asking myself, "What would I want if I were retiring?" Consider the number of people who can contribute monetarily toward a gift and plan accordingly. Imagine if twenty people gave twenty dollars, then you would have four hundred dollars for her gift.

Cruise

If she enjoys the beach, why not book a cruise for her? You can usually purchase an "off-season" ticket for little to nothing. On the day of the party, give her a "goody basket" with a new beach towel, sunscreen, and a great Christian novel to read, and when she says, "What's this for?" you can tell her!

Monogrammed Blanket

Add her hire and retire date and a sentiment such as "May your sweet memories keep you warm" on the blanket to turn it into a great keepsake.

Engraved Jewelry

What lady wouldn't want a beautiful watch with her retirement date engraved on the back? Or a gorgeous strand of pearls with her initials on the clasp?

Year at the Spa

Don't we all fantasize about our retiring one day and living the life of luxury? Purchasing a year's supply of manicures or other treatments at the spa can make that dream a reality.

SAMPLE ITINERARY

Welcome	Special Scripture Readings
Blessing	Popcorn Prayer
Dinner	Favorite Song
Roast	Video
Skit	Helium Balloons—Outside!
Opening the Gifts	

Up, Up, and Away

As you give this party, you're giving your coworker a wonderful opportunity to say good-bye to the work setting. She'll leave this party knowing that she is cared for and appreciated. She will have something to look forward to as she embarks on the next season of her life. After all, life does happen after work!

YVETTE THOMAS is a minister's wife, mother of three, and Women's Director at Rehoboth Baptist Church in Atlanta, Georgia, where she and her family reside. Raised around her family's restaurant (Ann's Diner) in Callahan, Florida, she's had a lot of practice cooking. Gatherings at her home focus on Jesus, surprise, and wonder! Yvette is a speaker and freelance writer.

Office Events

C ANDY A RRINGTON

W ITH OUR HURRIED, busy lives, it's sometimes difficult to plan and schedule a nice dinner for our immediate family members, much less an entire office staff. Often, coordinating an office event is viewed as a necessary drudgery and evokes little enthusiasm or creativity on the part of the planners. While the task may seem monumental, there are a number of things you can do to make the event less stressful for you and enjoyable to all.

When approaching the planning of an office event, consider the eupeptic question, "What is the best way to eat an elephant?" The answer, of course, is one bite at a time. Planning an office party is similar. By dividing each task into bite-size chunks, you'll be more likely to swallow and digest the whole project without a bad case of indigestion.

Consider the following ways to carve the task at hand into manageable bites:

Think Ahead

Many seasonal events require you to think a year or more in advance of the actual party date to secure off-property locations and/or catering services.

Large corporations usually book facilities from one year to another, often making it difficult to get on the calendar of a popular location. If you're trying to gain a spot at such a facility, make contact roughly fifteen to eighteen months prior to the date you hope to reserve. Businesses that hesitated in reserving a slot or change dates provide an opening for you to book the location. Similarly, with summer events, allow up to a year prior to the target date.

Avoid Procrastination

When the big event is months away on the calendar, it is tempting to put off preparations. Resist the urge. Getting as much as possible done in the early planning stages of an event will help relieve pressure as the date approaches. You can never foresee the unexpected and waiting until the eleventh hour almost invites a fiasco. There are always illnesses, scheduling conflicts, or last-minute work deadlines looming in the wings, waiting to take center stage and send your production to the thumbs down category of the critic's column. Working out the little details well in advance of the event ensures that the show goes on without a hitch if your understudy has to step in at the last minute.

Delegate

If you're of the mind-set that something can't be done correctly unless you handle it yourself, get over that pattern of thinking. While you want to maintain a certain level of control, delegating is a good thing. If you're working with a committee, spend some time talking to the members and discovering their strengths and talents. A good way to do this is to ask them their previous experiences in planning similar events or determine what life experiences lend themselves to expertise in a particular area. For instance, you may find that one of your committee members is a Master Gardener who has talent not only with floral creations, but also with table decorating. This person may even have photos of her floral and table designs. Think of the potential of giving her responsibility for this aspect of the event.

Determine the Nature of the Event

Who is your target audience? Is the event officewide or only for management? Will the party include spouses or other adult guests? Is it primarily an appreciation event for clients or is it family-oriented? The answers to these questions will determine the direction you take.

Gearing the event toward families opens up a number of opportunities to secure locations that are more entertainment-oriented. My husband's company has scheduled Saturday family events at a theme park or state park. The theme park was less than a two-hour drive away and included a substantially reduced admission price and a free meal. Other than gathering for the meal, families were able to explore the park on their own. The state park outing was similar—within an hour's drive, picnic lunch provided under several large tents, and free admission to hike and view the scenery.

Consider Location

Often it is assumed that a money savings will result by having an in-house function, but this is not always the case. By the time you add in cleaning the office (and many times it requires cleaning beyond the usual service to make it "party-worthy"), procuring extra tables and chairs, and hiring additional staff, you may find it more cost-effective to go with a functional, well-organized off-site event.

Having a party in your office is very much akin to having a party in your home. Since you "live" in your office, you'll need some extra time and elbow grease to shine it up to an acceptable status, even if the guests are your own employees.

One events coordinator thought she had everything ready for an in-house company Christmas party for families. A game room, complete with magician, was set up for the children; the swan ice sculpture made it to the table without a broken neck or melted wing; the cleaning crew had done their thing; and the caterer arrived on time. However, as the setting sun shined through the front glass doors and surrounding wall panels, she saw the greasy handprints of thousands of visitors. Less than an hour prior to party time, the coordinator, in holiday attire, was busy with a squeegee doing last-minute cleaning.

In addition, most employees and managers have trouble moving into a social mode in a traditionally professional setting. As a result, in-house events can turn out to be rather stiff, formal affairs despite efforts to make them otherwise. It is unrealistic to expect an easy transition to a party frame of mind when surrounded by various trappings of the 9-to-5 job.

Planning for smaller groups allows more flexibility. Sometimes an owner may even opt to have the event at her home. While the gesture may be well intended, this may cause feelings of "us" and "them" with employees. Some employees may be left feeling their own financial inferiority after being in the posh home of the company president or department head. Sticking to neutral ground often promotes better relations. Local hotels or restaurants with private dining rooms are a good option.

A word of caution about off-site locations: I once opted to host an event at a horse farm in a nice log cabin designed specifically for parties. I thought people would enjoy an afternoon in the country. What I failed to realize was the unwillingness of some to venture to an unknown location. Even though I had a head count prior, only about seven people showed up and we were left with quadruple the amount of food needed. The local homeless shelter had a feast that day.

Lesson learned: If you decide to use a remote location, consider meeting at the office to caravan or carpool and do a really good job with directions and maps.

Consider these creative location options in planning: art museums, aquariums, municipal airports, lakeside retreats, park shelters, or aboard a boat or ferry.

Whether the location is in-house or off-site, carefully consider traffic flow. It is important to calculate ahead of time how people will circulate in the space available. This is particularly important if people are moving from a central location into another area to go through a serving line. If there is a band and dance floor, you need to keep the flow for that activity in mind. Channeling plate-laden individuals to tables across a crowded dance floor invites disaster. Also, if people are moving to various anterior rooms from the central location, you're going to need signage or a person positioned to direct traffic from one room to another.

Select the Food

While you can't fit everyone's needs, it is good to provide a variety. My husband and I are both allergic to shellfish. He is also diabetic. We've been in situations where the main course was shrimp, with no option, followed by an extensive dessert bar with no fresh fruit. While we didn't especially mind making a meal of salad, bread, and a vegetable, the evening could have been different if those planning the dinner had considered that not everyone could eat seafood and sugar.

Raw vegetables and fruits are always a good item to add to the menu. While it is interesting to go with an unusual or theme-related menu, make sure that you include items that are palatable to a large number of people. Caterers can provide a number of options within a specific price range. Generally, it works more smoothly to let them handle everything.

Legal Issues Regarding Alcohol

Hopefully, the majority of individuals have moved beyond the line of think-ing that social interaction and drinking are synonymous. In addition to the Biblical warnings about the pitfalls of strong drink, employers are now legally liable for injuries resulting from employee consumption of too much alco-hol at a company function. Of course, the best plan is not to serve alcohol at all, but if you do, consider these steps to safeguard you and your employees.

- State company policy regarding alcohol prior to the event.
- Have a cash bar with a bartender rather than an open, serve-yourself arrangement.
- Use a hand stamp system that allows persons no more than three drinks during the event.
- Provide plenty of nonalcoholic drinks and lots of food.
- Encourage managers to set a positive example by not drinking.

Preview Entertainment

If entertainment is going to be a part of the event, make sure you get refer-ences or actually preview the entertainment before signing a contract. Promotional material does exactly what it implies—promotes. Previewing or getting references helps avoid unwanted surprises.

Possible entertainment options include: a band, a DJ, a magician, or a local choral group.

Invitations

Many event planners have discovered the effective use of electronic invita-tions with a reply-by date. These e-mail invitations work especially well in large companies and help planners get a more accurate count. Don't forget to snail mail invitations to retirees who are traditionally invited to gatherings.

If you opt to distribute invitations through regular interoffice mail, make sure that you include a reply-by date on these as well. In general, about 40 percent of the number invited show up.

Feedback

Getting a critique of the event is something we tend to shy away from, but in the long run, it is helpful in providing information for future planning. Select a few employees to talk with once the event is over, or if you're feeling brave, distribute a comment card during the party.

Don't Mess with a Good Thing

If you pull off an event that consistently gains rave reviews, stick with it. While you may want to experiment with various aspects of the event, keep the core intact. One event planner for a large engineering firm stated, "I always know Charlie's Barbecue is going to be a hit with the employees. The quality of the food is consistently good. They do all the setup, serving, and cleanup and I never get anything but positive comments from our folks."

Budget-saving Tips

Use Your Resources

Something that may be overlooked is the ability to benefit from connections when securing off-site locations, caterers, or entertainment. Clubhouses may be available to members free of charge or at a greatly reduced cost, so make it a point to know who among you has access to such locations. One event planner was able to secure an exclusive clubhouse facility free of charge because several company employees were residents of the community. The savings to the event's budget allowed her to hire a much-sought-after band as entertainment for the evening.

Network

In addition to using resources inside your company, networking with other company event planners is also advantageous. Talk about what has and hasn't worked and pool your ideas. Benefit from the creativity of others and be willing to think outside the box.

Consider Quality Versus Cost

As with most things, a bargain really isn't a bargain if the quality ends up being substandard. Choosing a menu, location, or entertainment based simply on dollar amount has the potential to leave you embarrassed and the office staff disappointed. Realize that the cheapest price may equal less than wonderful and make decisions accordingly. If you find you need to cut the budget, do it somewhere other than with the food. It's obvious when you scrimp on food and everyone will remember.

Employ Comparison Shopping

One of the best ways to make a decision when purchasing a service is to have several options to evaluate. It may be a little like comparing apples and oranges but come up with some sort of a system to tally the services provided and the cost. Don't make the comparison so broad that it is mind boggling. Three to four is plenty.

Watch for Hidden Costs

Make sure you understand all the costs involved with various aspects of the event. Ask caterers and others for an itemized list of charges and go over it carefully. One company thought it was getting the use of a room at a local museum free. However, planners failed to ask and later discovered that an upgrade to a larger room carried a fee.

CANDY ARRINGTON is a freelance writer whose publishing credits include *Writer's Digest, The Christian Communicator, CBN.com, Focus on the Family, Focus on Your Child, Discipleship Journal,* and *Christian Home & School.* She is coauthor with David W. Cox of *Aftershock: Help, Hope, and Healing in the Wake of Suicide* (Broadman & Holman Publishers, 2003). Candy lives in Spartanburg, South Carolina.

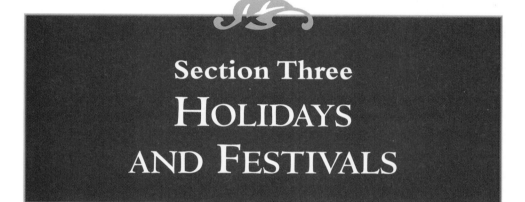

Section Three

HOLIDAYS
AND FESTIVALS

23

CHAPTER

Gifts from the Heart

SHERRY TAYLOR CUMMINS

WALK INTO my home right now and you will see it decorated in what I lovingly call "early gift." There's a small glass piano with a 22-karat-gold edge, a special gift from my father to show support during a difficult time. On the walls are framed prints from my church family, showing love and appreciation. The small candles are gifts from my mother, reminding me of peace and light. My two favorite gifts are from the hands of my grown children, created when they were in elementary school—a matted and framed portrait of me drawn by my daughter in crayon and an essay written by my son about why he loves me.

I cannot bring myself to retire these gifts because they hold such meaning to me. Each gift is significant in a unique way because each came from a unique and giving heart.

Why Give

God first gave to you. He gave the supreme gift, his beloved Son. He blesses you daily with tangible gifts such as life, shelter, and nourishment. God also

> ## TABITHA, REFLECTING GOD'S LIGHT
>
> Tabitha, a disciple of Christ, "was always doing good and helping the poor" (Acts 9:36–43). As you read the story of Tabitha and how her death affected people, you see that her giving was a shining light. She reflected God's love through that light. Her gifts went far beyond her good works, deep into the lives of those who received her gifts.

blesses you with intangible gifts such as hope, spiritual gifts, and love. The greater your depth of realization of God's love for you, the greater your desire to give to others. James wrote, "Every good and perfect gift is from above, coming down from the Father of the heavenly lights" (James 1:17).

Heartfelt giving is an opportunity to shine your light into the lives of others. "Let your light shine before men, that they may see your good deeds and praise your Father in heaven" (Matt. 5:16).

The Giving Way

You are to give from your heart, humbly, cheerfully, and with purpose. Matthew writes, "So when you give to the needy, do not announce it with trumpets, as the hypocrites do in the synagogues and on the streets, to be honored by men. I tell you the truth, they have received their reward in full" (Matt. 6:2). Don't give to get recognition; give so that God gets recognition. Paul writes, "God loves a cheerful giver" (2 Cor. 9:7b). Give, not out of obligation, but out of your love for God.

Gifts of the heart involve sacrifice. As a busy woman, you're well aware of the sacrifice of time that giving requires. If you find the sacrifice of giving a challenge, pray to God that He will make a way for you and provide you the resources to give. Pray that He molds for you a giving heart.

THIS COUPON OR CERTIFICATE IS REDEEMABLE FOR . . .[1]

Driving Carpool . . . Your turn becomes mine!

Washing the Dog . . . Glue a hotel sized soap here!

An Afternoon of Yard Work . . . Glue a seed packet to this one!

A Weekend of Baby-Sitting—Or One Baby-Sitting Job . . . in a diaper pin to this coupon!

One Weekend Away at Home . . . This is great for a husband or wife to give to each other, especially if the budget is really tight and even if it isn't.

I'll Arrange Everything . . . The calendar, the baby-sitting (trade this with another couple), what we'll do, and the menu too!

Help with the Clutter—Basement, Closets, or Garage . . . You need a partner for this!

Mending . . . Glue a needle and thread on this coupon!

Three Hours of a Helping Hand . . . You choose.

A Picnic . . . You pick the time and place.

An Old-Fashioned Pot Roast Dinner for Eight . . . Invite the people, pick the date!

A Pasta Dinner for Six . . . You pick the time and friends, I'll "maka" the pasta!

"Each one should use whatever gift he has received to serve others, faithfully administering God's grace in its various forms" (1 Peter 4:10).

—Dolley Carlson, *Christmas Gifts from the Heart*

The Blessings of Giving

There are two sides to the blessings of giving—blessings for the receiver and blessings for the giver. I truly enjoy receiving a gift, particularly a surprise gift. I feel blessed—encouraged and uplifted—that someone took the time to think of me in a special way. But the most uplifting moments are when I give to someone else. The stirring in my heart is exciting. I feel closer to God when I give. As my spirit sings with the gladness of giving, those around me also reap the joy!

Types of Giving

Gifts come in many types of packages. Some are elaborately packaged with satin and tulle, the beauty of it is a gift in itself. Others are packaged in spirit, unseen by human eyes and viewed through the resulting blessings. We give gifts at traditional times during holidays and celebrations devoted to family, friends, and beliefs. We give gifts at other times to show our love, care, and concern. We give gifts to celebrate new life, to show honor for lives that have moved into the next realm, and to comfort those they have left behind.

Gift Ideas

With the vast selection of stores, catalogs, and online venues, selecting the perfect gift for your family, friends, and coworkers can be a bit difficult. Today, there are many more holidays and celebrations on which we have placed the "need" for purchasing gifts, but thankfully, the social practice of gift giving today is also a much simpler process. Though we still have the tendency to agonize over gifts for every Hallmark occasion, the practice of gift giving only requires a couple of effortless actions from the gift giver—consideration and selection.

Whether the gift is for a family member or friend, illustrating your love and respect for them is the primary reason for your generosity. Gifts can also

---

STOP, LOOK, AND LISTEN[2]

Stop, even if it's just for a moment. It's hard to assess needs when you're in constant motion.

Look around. Who needs help, encouragement, or a "walking along-side" friend (that's you) bearing a caring gift from the heart?

Listen between the lines for fatigue, hopelessness, overwhelm, or loneliness and then . . . go to the Lord in prayer and ask Him to guide your steps and heart in the right direction.

"We have different gifts, . . . if it is serving, let him serve; if it is teaching, let him teach; if it is encouraging, let him encourage; if it is contributing to the needs of others, let him give generously; if it is leadership, let him govern diligently; if it is showing mercy, let him do it cheerfully" (Rom. 12:6–8).

—Dolley Carlson, *Friendship Gifts from the Heart*

---

demonstrate your appreciation and reverence for a coworker, and should be considered for holidays and other special occasions.

When considering the "perfect gift," always try and observe the personal preferences of the intended recipient(s). Many times, just in casual conversation, people will mention ideas for that ideal gift . . . pay attention . . . take notes.

Selecting just the right gift, one that shows the receiver how you feel about them, is most important. For any gift, you need to consider the type of relationship that exists between you and the recipient. For instance, you might

---

[2]©2001 by Dolley Carlson, *Friendship Gifts from the Heart*. Copied with permission by Cook Communications Ministries, p. 22. May not be further reproduced. All rights reserved.

consider getting a personalized gift for a coworker or client, though personalized gift giving can be appropriate for many other holidays and celebrations as well, including baby showers, anniversaries, and weddings. Specialty gift catalogs and Internet venues are excellent resources for purchasing that special gift.

No matter what the occasion, sometimes finding gifts that people will enjoy and appreciate is close to impossible. What's a solution? Gift certificates. Their simplicity and flexibility make them a perfect gift.

Other Quick and Easy Ways to Shine His Light

Touch the heart of the receiver with the gift of the written word—a poem, a letter, or just a note to let someone know that you care—it's lasting and valuable. Keep stamped note cards handy just for such occasions. Use early morning time or part of your lunch to jot a quick note and drop in the mail.

Food is always a welcome gift. Our earliest memories of warmth and security are tied to food. The sick, shut-ins, those in grief—there are many who would appreciate a gift of food. Homemade is great, but today we are blessed with so many retailers who create close-to-homemade delectables. Tasty breads, fresh cookies, even soup can be purchased on your way home from work. When people are ill or grieving, they may not feel much like eating. Rare is it when a person can't be sustained with a bowl of soup, even with little appetite. Your gift of a bowl of soup with warm bread will be just the thing!

It's a Wrap

The best part of giving a gift is the wrap. Make a gift-giving toolbox (filled with discount store bargains). Items might include tulle, satin ribbon, organza ribbon, newspaper, discount gift wrap, plain brown wrap, silk flowers, dried flowers, scissors, tape, glue, and any other tidbits you think may come in handy for a quick wrap.

Buy baskets and other containers at bargain prices off-season and use them to hold jars of soup and loaves of bread. Dress cookies up by putting them on "dollar-store" plates, wrap in plastic and tie with a big ribbon bow. Stock colored bags of all sizes to hold small gifts wrapped in tissue. Be creative and have fun. Get a routine that's helpful to you and keep your tools handy.

FRIENDSHIP TEA

This recipe is a delightful way to share friendship or to use as a party favor when wrapped in single serve portions. There are variations but this recipe can be given to your diabetic or carbohydrate-watching friends.

$1/2$ cup instant tea
1 cup powdered orange drink mix, sugar free
1 cup lemonade powder, sugar free
1 teaspoon cinnamon
1 teaspoon cloves

Combine ingredients and mix well. Empty into plastic bags and tie with ribbon. Add a tag that says, "Put 2 to 3 cups of mix in a mug and stir in 1 cup of boiling water." Recipe makes about 40 servings.

The Joy Box

The Joy Box is a box given to someone who is in special need of encouragement. A dear friend and the busiest person I know, Joanne, has made this one of her giving ministries. There is a small investment of time at the beginning, but if you create an assembly line process and do a little as time permits, you can continuously send joy to those around you.

MATERIALS: One shoe box; seven small, inexpensive gifts (soaps, candles, emery boards, playing cards, etc.); wrapping paper; tissue paper; a pill bottle; seven strips of paper each with a Scripture written out on it; brown shipping paper; mailing tape; and postage.

DESCRIPTION: Wrap the shoe box in wrapping paper, the lid and bottom separately. Roll each strip of Scripture paper around a pencil to shape and then drop into the pill bottle. Put the pill bottle into the box. Wrap each gift separately in tissue paper and place in the box. Place the Joy Box poem on top with instructions to take a "pill" from the bottle and open one gift each day for seven days. Feel free to create your own poem or note about what you want to convey to the receiver with the Joy Box, such as how you hope it brings them joy as you're remembering them each day in prayer. Wrap in brown paper, label, and mail. Look at Romans 15:13, Colossians 1:11, Philemon 1:20, Philemon 1:7, 1 Thessalonians 3:9 as examples of appropriate Scriptures.

A JOY BOX FOR YOU

A joy box for you to brighten your way
For this week one gift to open each day.
The great Physician has offered the cure.
You must take your pills to know it for sure.
So enjoy this token of our love for you,
For all that you are and all that you do.
We know no one else who brings us such joy, as you,
God's servant of purity and joy.
Enjoy these gifts and remember each day,
How we love and appreciate your way.

Giving of the Heart

God gave first to you. He blesses you daily. Shine your light and reflect His love to others through your giving. Be ready for opportunities that He brings your way. Keep tools for gift wrapping handy, shop for fillers and small gifts as you go, look for off-season prices and one-of-a-kind offers.

Remember that the most important gifts are those that we cannot see—friendship, time, love, forgiveness, and hope. True giving involves the heart, sacrifice, and a desire to please God. Enjoy the blessings of giving.

SHERRY TAYLOR CUMMINS is a freelance writer with contributions published in *Hearts at Home* magazine and faith-based anthologies. She works in Human Resources, Training and Leadership Development in Ann Arbor, Michigan. Sherry has two grown children, a son-in-law, and two beautiful grandchildren. Sherry is currently working on her first novel.

Valentine's Day

KAY HARMS

AH, VALENTINE'S DAY. The day that, according to florists, greeting card companies, and confectioners of everything sweet, I can revel in the attention of my sweetheart. According to these creators of tangible sweet sentiments, I can count on my husband, children, and cherished friends to do more than just "rise up and call me blessed." I can expect them to shower me with long-stemmed roses, creamy candy, gushy cards, and sparkling jewelry.

Right?!

Actually my first Valentine's Day as a new bride *was* quite spectacular. My eager-to-please husband sent me roses at work and had more flowers awaiting me at home. He also delighted me with a heart-shaped frozen yogurt pie, a box of chocolates, and a romantic dinner. But as my coworkers were quick to warn me, I could expect much less the next year. As the years passed, I must admit, I began to feel more disappointed than loved as each Valentine's Day proved less and less spectacular.

Perhaps you have also become disillusioned with this holiday of love. Perhaps you would just as soon mark this day off the calendar.

LOVELY NOTABLES

- Americans probably began exchanging handcrafted valentines in the early 1700s.
- In the 1840s, Esther Howland began selling the first mass-produced valentines in America.
- An estimated one billion valentine cards are sent each year, making Valentine's Day the second largest card-sending holiday of the year.
- Women purchase 85 percent of all valentines. (According to www.HistoryChannel.com.)

Would you like to know the secret to enjoying Valentine's Day? *It's a matter of focus.* Where is your focus on this red-letter day? Do you anticipate what others will do for you or are you busy planning a special day for the "somebodies" in your life? Will you be envious of the roses your office assistant receives, or will you plan to give her a single red rose for being such a loyal employee? Do you expect your husband to arrange for a sitter, take you to a posh restaurant, and surprise you with diamonds, or will you plan a special supper for your family followed by a romantic dessert for two?

"Do nothing out of selfish ambition or vain conceit," Paul wrote in Philippians 2:3, "but in humility consider others better than yourselves." Yet, if we are not wary of the misleading television commercials and magazine advertisements, as women we are tempted to think primarily of ourselves on this particular holiday.

Paul continues in verse four, "Each of you should look not only to your own interests, but also to the interests of others." If I concentrate *completely* on how I can express love, friendship, and appreciation to the important people in my life on Valentine's Day, I feel more satisfied and fulfilled as the day comes to a close, regardless of how others have expressed (or not expressed) those sentiments to me.

This year, why not make it your focus to express your love and appreciation to your sweetheart, family, friends, and coworkers through creative gifts, moments, and acts of gratitude? You may find, with a change of focus, that all your valentine dreams really do come true.

Focus on Being Prepared

Like all special occasions, Valentine's Day requires some forethought and planning. I have found that there are some things I can do throughout the year that keep me prepared for a festive Valentine's Day celebration.

- Purchase a large plastic tub for storing Valentine's Day supplies. When you put your Christmas tubs back in storage, take your valentine tub out of storage and put it where it will be more accessible as you approach February 14.
- Watch for Christmas items, such as strands of white lights, red paper plates and napkins, and red velvet bows, which can serve double duty as Valentine's Day accessories.
- Be alert throughout the year for items that can be used creatively on Valentine's Day: red or pink ribbon, CDs of classic love songs, silk rose petals, pretty candles and candle holders, a red-checked table cloth, and books of poetry.
- Look for items in heart-shaped varieties. Every February, new novelty items pop up in stores that can lend fun and whimsy to your celebration. Purchase a few each year that can be used over and over.

Focus on Family

Kids love Valentine's Day. They tend to approach this holiday with a sweet attitude worth emulating. Children get excited about making valentines for their classmates, friends, and teachers. They will go the extra mile to show Mom

Intense love does not measure, it just gives. —MOTHER TERESA

The following items often come in heart-shaped varieties and can make Valentine's Day fun for the whole family:

- Cookie cutters
- Waffle irons
- Pancake molds
- Cake pans
- Ice cube trays
- Paper doilies
- Confetti

and Dad how much they are loved. They still believe Valentine's Day is about *expressing* love rather than *receiving* high-priced roses, candy, and jewelry.

We can foster this kind and giving attitude by making Valentine's Day a special family day. We can teach them that romance is great, but family loyalty is of a higher value. We can show them that admirers are flattering, but true friends are hard to come by and worth keeping.

I have tried, even though my children are entering those emotional teenage years, to keep "romance" out of their celebration of Valentine's Day. There will be time for that later. While my children are young and at home, I want to use these years to establish a worthy celebration of true love—God's love. So I try to focus our Valentine's Day traditions around celebrating God's love for us, our love for each other as a family, and our love for our friends.

To accomplish my goal, I concentrate on making Valentine's Day very fun. And there are so many ways to make this day a blast for children of all ages. For instance, consider starting the day with a "hearty" breakfast. Waffles, pancakes, toast, eggs, and biscuits can all be made in the shape of hearts with the right equipment. Fluffy, heart-shaped biscuits filled with raspberry jam are a personal favorite, but crepes with strawberries and powdered sugar are even more festive.

When you're packing lunches for school children or a working husband, cut their sandwiches with a large heart-shaped cookie cutter. Don't forget to write a sweet sentiment or a "lovely" Bible verse on their napkin, too.

> "Greater love has no one than this, that he lay down his life for his friends."
> (John 15:13)

If your kids get home in the afternoon before you do, you may want to leave them a special snack to enjoy before dinner. Heart-shaped cookies, even store-bought, taste better on this love-centered day. You can set out a tub of vanilla icing, red food coloring, and a plastic knife or two so your children can frost their own sugar cookies.

For a "sweet" game, set out the family's checkerboard, but put away the red and black checkers. Instead, put a bowl of Hershey's Hugs® and Hershey's Kisses® beside the board with instructions to use these candies to play the game, allowing the players to *eat* their opponent's "checkers" when they jump them. They can also play tic-tac-toe with these chocolates.

Finally, dinnertime can be a celebration of family love at its best. In a day when many families are broken into fragments due to loss, separation, and divorce, your family can offer a special valentine to another family on this emotion-packed night. Whether your family is a traditional mom, pop, and kids unit, a blended household, or a single-parent family, you have something to give to someone else that may feel left out, abandoned, or hurting on February 14.

With your family's input, invite another family or single person to join you for a relaxed evening at home. With your kitchen table and family room festively decorated from the items in your valentine storage tub, you lay aside all facades and be yourselves on this casual evening. Build a fire, turn on some jazzy music or praise songs, set out some board games, and tell everybody to take off their shoes.

Perhaps you will set out the ingredients for make-your-own pizzas. Or you could let everyone build his or her own tacos, chilidogs, or omelets. After dinner, you might even get daring enough to bring out the ice cream and fixings for sundaes. Just keep it simple and easy. The focus tonight is on

> A friendship can weather most things and thrive in thin soil; but it needs a little mulch of letters and phone calls and small, silly presents every so often—just to save it from drying out completely.[1] —PAM BROWN

showing love and hospitality to someone who might otherwise be feeling unloved and unwanted.

As you put forth a little extra effort to make this day special for your family and another family in need of a boost, you will find your focus drifting away from yourself and toward the needs of others. Additionally, you will be teaching your children that love is not self-centered, but other-centered.

Focus on Friendship

Valentine's Day is also a great opportunity to express love to girlfriends.

Depending on the day of the week and your schedule, you may choose from a variety of creative ways to express your valentine sentiments to a close friend or coworker. The objective is simple: to do *something* that is out of the ordinary for *someone* who is out of the ordinary.

On a workday, when time is of the essence, a simple recognition of a coworker, supervisor, neighbor, or friend speaks volumes. Consider the following ideas for making this Valentine's Day memorable.

Mug 'n Muffin

Prepare a tasty batch of muffins the night before February 14. Wrap them individually in pretty pink or red cellophane and tie them up with curled ribbon. Place the wrapped muffins in novelty coffee mugs that express sentiments of friendship. (Or you may opt for a mug with a silly quip about

---

[1] Pam Brown, BrainyQuote, 27 December 2003, <http://www.brainyquote.com/quotes/authors/p/pam_brown.html> (27 December 2003).

chocolate or coffee!) Now you're prepared to share a coffee break and a simple gift with one or more friends.

Lunch for Two

It's not unusual for coworkers to grab lunch together, so you will need to be a little creative if you want this lunch break to convey valentine wishes. Consider packing a picnic lunch for you and a friend. (You don't have to eat your picnic outside; your office, her cubby, or even the lunchroom will do nicely.) Include individual servings of pasta salad, croissant sandwiches, fruit, and a sweet finale. Don't forget the cloth napkins, a tablecloth, and silverware. These are the special touches that show how much you care.

Walk'n Talk

Perhaps you and your coworker are trying to save your daily allowance of calories for the evening meal. Instead of lunching at noon, ask your friend to join you for a brisk walk. While you burn those calories, warm your pal's heart by thanking her for her friendship. If you work it just right, you can plan a cappuccino or frozen yogurt break at the halfway mark.

Focus on Romance

So far we've looked at Valentine's Day as a fun-filled family day and an occasion to celebrate friendship, but we certainly don't want to neglect romance completely. After all, most of us need to take advantage of every possible excuse for a little romance.

With work, parenting, church involvement, and household obligations, we often find ourselves too busy or too tired to ignite the sparks of romance. But here is your opportunity to plan a romantic moment with your personal signature all over it.

Keep in mind that romance need not be so narrowly defined as a candlelit dinner and dancing. According to the dictionary, romance simply includes anything that lends to being sentimental, expressive, extravagant, and loving. In other words, romance is that which takes us out of the ordinary so that we are prompted to express our deepest sentiments toward another person in a loving and extravagant way.

This Valentine's Day, why not consider a fresh approach to romance? Spend some time brainstorming on settings, activities, decorations, foods, and music that tend to put you and your sweetheart in a romantic frame of mind. Remember that your relationship is unique and the elements that build romance for the two of you are unique as well. Perhaps a moonlit stroll with a flashlight and a thermos of hot chocolate is right for you and your honey. Maybe the two of you prefer dessert in bed with candlelight and soft music setting the mood. Then again, you might opt for a late dinner for two, sitting on the floor at your coffee table with only a roaring fire to serenade you.

Just keep in mind that true intimacy usually begins with talking—sharing feelings, dreams, concerns, and passions. As you plan the romantic part of your Valentine's Day, include the time and the right atmosphere for relaxed conversation.

Finally, watch your focus. Even as you enter into the romantic phase of your Valentine's Day, whether it is a breakfast in bed or a late-night dance in your socks, make it your goal to please rather than be pleased. In giving of yourself and thinking of your true love's feelings above your own, you will find the true satisfaction of a Valentine's Day well spent.

KAY HARMS, though busy as a freelance writer, public speaker, pastor's wife and mother, still loves to open her home to others. Kay grew up in Georgia where her mother taught her the benefits and the how-to's of southern hospitality. She lives in Mabank, Texas, where hospitality is alive and well.

Easter

DAPHNE SMITH

EASTER IS one of the few holidays with a true spiritual history. Many of the symbols we use during Easter have specific meaning. It is a great time to share with children and friends why we use and do the things we do. The following is a brief list of Easter symbols that have direct ties to Christianity.

- **Eggs** are a symbol of new life and resurrection.
- **Easter lilies** are a reminder of Jesus coming back to life. The trumpet shape of the flower announces His return.
- **Crosses** are symbols of our Christian faith.
- **White clothes or new clothes** are worn because of the tradition of baptism at Easter. Baptism represents a new life.
- **Lambs** represent the Lamb of God.

Timing

One of the challenges in pulling off your extravaganza is that Easter can fall anytime between March 22 and April 25. Based on your geographical location

---

JELLY BEAN SIGNIFICANCE

Red represents the blood He gave.
Green represents the grass He made.
Yellow represents the sun so bright.
Orange represents the edge of night.
· Black represents the sins that are made.
White represents the grace He gave.
Purple represents the hour of sorrow.
Pink represents the new tomorrow.

---

and Mother Nature, you could be hunting for eggs in the snow. I remember on more than one occasion wearing flannel and searching for eggs with my sisters in the living room. And we grew up in Texas. Since Easter is a spring event, an outdoor celebration can be fantastic. Just make sure the weather will allow everyone to be comfortable outside—and have a backup plan for peace of mind.

Time of day is also a consideration for your celebration. Will you have enough time in advance to prepare if you want to welcome your guests right after your worship service? Or would it be better to have your meal later in the day? Are you willing to allow others to bring dishes to share? This can save you quite a bit of time and give you more time to focus on other aspects of your event.

Setting and Decorations

Imagine everyone gathering around tables outdoors decorated with ivy and miniature clay pots. Each pot can have the guest's name on it to serve as a place card. The pots can be filled with anything from jelly beans to dyed eggs to fresh or silk flowers. A buffet table with an Easter lily as your centerpiece can keep the atmosphere casual. Outdoor celebrations are welcoming to children and a terrific tribute to all living things.

For a more elegant affair, the celebration can be brought indoors. Depending upon the number of guests, you might consider multiple seating areas using your dining room or kitchen table as a giant buffet. White table-cloths and bright cloth napkins will help bring the feeling of spring inside. A clear bowl or pedestal provides a way to show off dyed eggs that you and your children have created.

Another way to decorate your dining area is to tie eggs from the light fixture overhead. If you're using plastic eggs, use clear tape around the seam so that halves of eggs aren't falling into your food. If using real eggs, make a hole in each end of the egg with a needle. Make a larger hole in the larger end of the egg. Using the needle, break up the contents of the egg before blowing. Blow the yolk out of the larger hole. To clean the eggs, run water through the eggs and allow them to dry before decorating. Placing a dab of glue on the smaller hole will help prevent farther cracking. Cover the larger hole by gluing ribbon to the egg at that spot. Varying the lengths of ribbon for your egg chandelier will give the greatest visual impact.

Starting the Day

Be sure your morning is planned carefully, as your day will be very full of activity. Hot cross buns are a good way to start the morning. You can use this opportunity to point out to your family the significance of the white cross on the bun. Perhaps an overnight refrigerator casserole could be cooking while the first egg hunt of the day takes place.

One tradition I got to experience growing up was with my father. Every Easter morning he greeted me with, "Alleluia, the Lord is risen." My response was, "He is risen indeed, alleluia." To this day, my father and I call each other long distance to share this special part of the holiday.

While my father and I had our morning tradition, my mother was busy the night before with her tradition. Each Easter morning, we awoke to an Easter basket filled with goodies. Over the years, Mom tried several different basket fillers. She used everything from traditional plastic colored grass—a different color for each child's basket to latch hook rug yarn (not nearly as messy) and even paper shred.

Menu Ideas

Serving your meal outdoors lends itself to things like fresh lemonade and quiche. A fruit and vegetable tray, a tray of meats and cheeses and various rolls and breads allow your guests to meet their needs without you worrying about items being the right temperature. Cupcakes, carrot cake, and fruit-filled pies are all great outdoor desserts.

Being indoors can increase your menu options because you have the advantage of warming trays and a climate-controlled environment. Warm things will stay warmer longer and things like gelatin won't melt as quickly.

For starters, how about deviled eggs? The key is to remember that for safety, boiled eggs should be left out of the refrigerator for no more than two hours. Rhubarb has always been a family favorite at my house. Frozen rhubarb combined with tapioca, a little sugar, and lemon juice makes an easy make-ahead side dish combining sweet and tart flavors.

Our family usually serves leg of lamb for Easter. When buying the leg of lamb, choose one that weighs ten pounds or less. If it weighs more than ten pounds, it is considered mutton and will have a much stronger, gamier taste. Ham and brisket are also good ideas. All of these meats can be served to large crowds and can be cooking at a low temperature during worship services ready to serve upon returning home. The Easter feast is also a great time to enjoy asparagus. Served either cold, roasted, or warmed and drizzled with hollandaise, just about everyone will enjoy this versatile vegetable. Remember potatoes or bread for those who like heartier fare. In some areas of the country, Easter bread can be found. It can be easily made at home if time allows. For dessert, how about an angel food cake with strawberries and whipping cream? Making bunny- and lamb-shaped cakes is also a lot of fun and is a great way to get other family members involved. You may need to sacrifice perfect decorating for happy memories. Trust me, it will taste just as good.

Remember, the more eggs you dye, the more you have to deal with. If handled properly, hard-boiled eggs can last several days in the refrigerator. The eggs make great portable breakfasts and lunches. Deviled eggs and egg salad are also good ways to use them.

Activities

I recommend dyeing all eggs at least a day before the event. You can plan anything from an egg toss to egg rolling to an egg spoon relay. I would encourage you to use hard-boiled eggs for these activities.

Older teens can hide eggs for the younger children to find. To keep the little ones distracted during the hiding, they can make their own Easter baskets using plastic pint-sized berry baskets. Handles can be made from pipe cleaners. Be sure to put filler in the baskets to cushion their finds. Or, use

EASTER COOKIES

(To be made on Easter eve.)   1   cup sugar

1   cup whole pecans   Zippered plastic food bag

1   teaspoon vinegar   Wooden spoon

3   egg whites   Tape

     Pinch of salt, with a   Bible

     little extra

Preheat oven to 300 degrees.

1. Place pecans in the bag and let children beat them with the wooden spoon until small pieces. Read John 19:1–3.

2. Let each child smell the vinegar. Pour the vinegar into mixing bowl. Read John 19:28–30.

3. Add egg whites to the vinegar. Explain the eggs represent life. Read John 10:10, 11.

4. Sprinkle a little salt into each child's hand. Let them taste it. Add pinch to ingredients already in bowl. Read Luke 23:27.

5. Add sugar to other ingredients. Explain that the sweetest part of the Easter story is that Jesus died because He loves us. Read Psalm 34:8 and John 3:16.

6. Beat ingredients with a mixer on high speed for 12 to 15 minutes or until soft peaks form. Explain that the color white represents the purity of our lives through God's eyes of those whose sins have been cleansed by Jesus. Read Isaiah 1:18 and John 3:1–3.

7. Fold in broken nuts. Drop by teaspoonfuls onto wax paper-covered cookie sheet. Explain that each mound represents the rocky tomb where Jesus' body was laid. Read Matthew 27:57–60.

8. Put the cookie sheet in the oven. Close the door and turn the oven OFF. Give each child a piece of tape to seal the oven door. Read Matthew 27:65, 66.

(Continued)

9. Explain that the children might feel sad leaving the cookies in the oven overnight and all alone. Read John 16:20 and 22.
10. On Easter morning, open the oven and give everyone a cookie. Notice the cracked surface and take a bite. The cookies are hollow. On the first Easter, Jesus' followers were amazed to find the tomb open and empty. Read Matthew 28:1–9.

paper bags with handles. Have the children decorate the bags with markers, crayons, and stickers.

Limit the number of eggs each child is allowed to find during the hunt. That will help avoid hurt feelings and encourage the kids to help each other. The teens can join in for a hunt as well. The adults can hide coin-filled plastic eggs. It's a great way for the teens to enjoy the "thrill of the hunt" as well as earn a little loose change.

Another fun activity is to have an Easter bonnet-decorating contest. Paper plates, miscellaneous ribbons, recycled Christmas bows, tape, markers, and scissors are all you need. Have the children decorate the plates and then use ribbon stapled to either side of the plate's edge to create the ties. You may even get a parade out of it. For the young boys, you could use brown paper bags and have precut bowties available for decorating. The bowties can be taped onto their shirt collar, and they too will have something to show off.

When planning your *egg*stravaganza, remember that Jesus is the reason for this season too. Easter is about so much more than chocolate and bunnies. We have a terrific opportunity and I believe obligation to share our faith during this time. Sharing the glorious meaning of the holiday will serve to enrich and enhance its special purpose in our lives.

DAPHNE SMITH is a speaker and author living in Bentonville, Arkansas. Having moved from Dallas with her family, she discovered her passion for ministry in the foothills of the Ozarks. Allowing the *voice within* to guide her course, Daphne feels honored to have the responsibilities of her family and career.

26

CHAPTER

Fourth of July

MICHELLE MEDLOCK ADAMS

SINCE SEPTEMBER 11, 2001, Americans have become more patriotic. Suddenly, the national anthem means a little more when we stand and sing it at ball games. We now fly our American flags on more than just Flag Day. And, the Fourth of July has become a bigger celebration than ever before. Like the song says, "I'm proud to be an American," and I enjoy entertaining on that day.

What better way to celebrate the freedoms we enjoy in this country than by gathering with friends and family for an afternoon of food and fun? Whether you host a simple gathering of family and friends or a knockout neighborhood extravaganza, you'll need a party plan.

Get a Party Plan

First, you need to decide if you'll be doing all the cooking, if you'll hire a caterer, or if you'll host a pitch-in dinner. If your cash flow doesn't allow for a caterer, the pitch-in picnic is a fun way to go. Indicate on your invitations that you'll be providing the main dish (barbecue, hot dogs and hamburgers, etc.) and ask each family to bring a dessert, salad, or side dish. To avoid having thirteen green bean casseroles, ask guests to RSVP and indicate what dish they'll be bringing.

Fun Fourth Invitation

Have fun with your party invitations. Of course, you can simply get stars and stripes invitations from a retailer or online party place, or you can create your own designs. If you opt to create your own, here are some suggestions.

- Cut out invitations to look like Uncle Sam's hats.
- Make each invitation in the shape of a star.
- Make miniature flag invitations.

Write clever wording to entice your prospective guests. You might use something like this for your inside copy:

"Come celebrate the Fourth with us.
We'd love to have you come.
We'll party here from 1 to 5.
With food and folks and fun!"

Offer Fun Festivities for the Whole Family

If you have a swimming pool, you might host a Fourth of July pool party. The kids are sure to love a splish-splash bash. If you don't have a pool, don't worry. There are many other ways to entertain your guests. Here are some things sure to keep your party lively and fun:

Karaoke

If you don't have your own karaoke machine, you can rent one from most party places. There's nothing quite like a bunch of wannabe superstars singing songs and "busting a move" in front of giggling friends and family. What a hoot! You can buy karaoke tapes and CDs tailored specifically for your guests. So, if you'll be entertaining a group of thirty-somethings, '80s hits would be a winner. Get the idea?

Watermelon Seed-spitting Contest

Watermelon is in season in July, and who doesn't like to compete? You can feature an adult seed-spitting competition as well as a children's contest. Have gag gifts on hand for each super spitter—just to add to the fun of it all.

Bake-off

If you're hosting a big bash, why not have an apple pie bake-off? There's nothing more American than apple pie, and who doesn't love a little friendly competition? You could even make a patriotic ribbon to give to the grand-prize winner or go all out and have a little trophy or plaque made with a place to engrave the name of each year's winner. It could become a holiday tradition.

Neighborhood Pet Parade

Each year, our little neighborhood has a pet/kid Fourth of July parade. It's great fun. Children decorate their dogs, go-karts, bikes, and scooters, and some even make floats. Then, at a designated time, they parade around the neighborhood for all of the camera-carrying parents. It's a blast! You could start the same tradition in your neighborhood.

Put Some Kid-Friendly Fun into Your Fourth

There's nothing quite like a backyard barbecue on the Fourth of July—lots of food, lots of folks, and a whole lot of fun. You know what else abounds at a backyard barbecue? Children. You can count on it. So, you're going to need some fun activities to keep the kids happy. Here are four Fourth of July crafty activities to put some pizzazz into your party.

Finger-painting Fireworks

Using a separate poster board for each child or a large sheet for the entire group, encourage the kids to use various colors of paint to create a fireworks picture. Have them drop blobs of paint onto the poster board or sheet, and then have them use a spoon to swirl the paint in a circular motion. The end result? A painting that will look like fireworks bursting in the sky.

Lady Liberty Torch

Using old newspapers rolled into large cone shapes, ask the kids to paint the cones. Then, help the children stuff each torch with red, yellow, and orange tissue paper to create the flame of the torch. You can also help the kids make crowns, and then have a Lady Liberty parade around the yard.

Patriotic T-Shirts

Using white T-shirts and red and blue puffy paints, ask the kids to make a patriotic design such as a flag, fireworks, Lady Liberty, "I ♥ America," etc. Help the kids put their names, in puffy paint style, on the backs of their T-shirts.

Really Radical Rockets

Using construction paper, make a cone shape and ask the kids to decorate the cones with markers and patriotic stickers that you'll provide. Next, cut two-inch slits on opposite sides of the wide-open end. Then, use eighteen inches of string, and with the point up, put the string through the slits. Finally, pull firmly on the ends of the relaxed string and watch the rockets fly into the air.

Fourth Fixin's

If you're providing all of the food without the help of a caterer, keep it simple. It's too hot to spend your entire Fourth of July weekend in the kitchen.

Besides, you'd like to enjoy the party too, right? So, plan a menu with dishes you can fix ahead to make it easier on yourself the day of the party. For example, make a strawberry, white chocolate, and blueberry cheesecake. Or, make a banana split cake the day before, because it needs to chill overnight anyway. It's always a holiday favorite—no matter the festive occasion. Here's that recipe in case you don't have it. I've added a few "Michelle touches" for some oomph!

BANANA SPLIT CAKE MICHELLE STYLE

2	cups of flour	3	or 4 bananas
3	sticks of oleo	1	can of crushed pineapple
2	cups of chopped pecans	1	9-ounce Cool Whip
2	eggs	1	cup of chocolate chips
2	cups powdered sugar		Maraschino cherries
3	ounces of cream cheese (soft)		(optional)

Combine flour, 2 sticks of oleo, and 1 cup of chopped pecans and pat into the bottom of a 9 × 13 greased pan. Bake for 20 minutes at 350 degrees. Cool completely. Beat eggs, sugar, another stick of oleo, and cream cheese for 10 minutes, and place on top of crust. Slice a layer of bananas over the mixture, and top with pineapple. Next, spread Cool Whip over the top. Sprinkle with remaining chopped pecans and cherries and chocolate chips, and refrigerate overnight before serving.

Need some additional ideas for Fourth of July food? Here are some shortcuts I often use when entertaining. Go to a warehouse club and purchase the mini-quiches, the pre-rolled frozen meatballs, a cheese ball or two with crackers, miniature egg rolls, cheese sticks, hot wings, and other such finger foods. These are easy—simply warm them up, and place them on your festive platters. For the meatballs, you'll need to bake them in a special sauce in order to hit a home run. See page 256 for the sauce recipe.

AMAZING MEATBALL SAUCE

1 can of jellied cranberry sauce	2 tablespoons of brown sugar
1 12-ounce bottle of chili sauce	1 tablespoon of lemon juice

Cook over medium heat until smooth, stirring constantly. Now, pour over meatballs and bake at 350 degrees for 30 minutes or so.

Of course, you can stick with the cookout theme, and simply serve hamburgers and hot dogs with chips, corn on the cob, etc. Or, you can jazz up the traditional burgers. Here's a quick recipe for baked hamburgers.

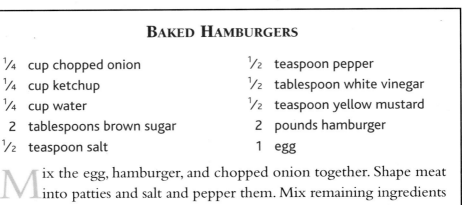

BAKED HAMBURGERS

¼ cup chopped onion	½ teaspoon pepper
¼ cup ketchup	½ tablespoon white vinegar
¼ cup water	½ teaspoon yellow mustard
2 tablespoons brown sugar	2 pounds hamburger
½ teaspoon salt	1 egg

Mix the egg, hamburger, and chopped onion together. Shape meat into patties and salt and pepper them. Mix remaining ingredients together over heat and stir constantly. Put patties into a casserole dish and pour the sauce over them. Bake 60 minutes. Serves about six. You can serve them on a bun or simply plain.

No matter what you serve, make sure you present each dish in a fun, festive way. Use stars and stripes centerpieces. Tie red, white, and blue balloons on the backs of each chair. Sprinkle silver and gold stars and confetti down the center of a white tablecloth. Slide miniature flags under each of

---

STRAWBERRY PUNCH

1	12-ounce can of frozen orange juice		1	12-ounce package of frozen strawberries
1	12-ounce can of frozen lemonade		3	packages of raspberry Kool-Aid
1	46-ounce can of pineapple juice		2	cups sugar
			3	quarts water
			2	quarts ginger ale or Seven-Up

Mix everything together except the strawberries and ginger ale and freeze. Remove from the freezer 60–90 minutes before serving. This time allows the mixture to get slushy. Add the 12-ounce package of strawberries and 2 quarts of ginger ale or Seven-Up. Serves about 50 people.

---

your napkin rings. Use red carnations, white daisies, and blue bonnets to make festive flower arrangements. Be creative and have fun!

Put Some Punch into Your Fourth Menu

My mother-in-law Martha (No, not Martha Stewart, but she might as well be!) makes the best strawberry punch. Sure, you probably have a similar recipe, but Martha presents hers in such a way that it tastes even better. It's slushy and very refreshing. Use it for every festive occasion that calls for punch. I do. Oh, and use pretty punch bowls and punch cups. You might even wish to place some fresh flowers around the bottom of the outside of the punch bowl for a decorative table presentation.

Remember Why We Celebrate

For an added touch, it's nice to take a few moments (right before the meal is served or right after) to read a portion of the Declaration of Independence signed on July 4, 1776, and pray for our governmental leaders today—local, state, and national. It's also nice to recognize any war veterans who might be in attendance, thanking them for fighting for and defending the freedoms that we enjoy today.

Also, you might read the Scripture found in 2 Chronicles 7:14: "If my people, who are called by my name, will humble themselves and pray and seek my face and turn from their wicked ways, then will I hear from heaven and will forgive their sin and will heal their land."

The Fourth of July is about more than just fireworks, apple pies, and parades. It's about thanking God for the freedoms we enjoy in this great nation, and praying for those who lead and defend America. So, in between watermelon bites, take time to celebrate the real meaning of the Fourth of July.

Celebrate Safely: Fireworks Safety Tips for a Fun Fourth

No Fourth of July is complete without a few fireworks, but be careful! Here are some safety tips to keep your Fourth festive and free from injury.

- Keep all fireworks in a closed box: Only take them out one at a time, and keep the box far away from smokers, the grill, and the firework display area.
- Follow the instructions: Read each firework label carefully before igniting. Make sure you know what to expect and how to execute.
- Light and run: Light the tip of the firework at arm's length (preferably with a safety firework lighter or fuse wick), and run away.
- Stay back: After lighting the firework, stand well back and make sure others do, too.
- Never return to an ignited firework: It could go off in your face.
- Never throw fireworks: It's too unpredictable as to where they might land.
- Keep a hose nearby: Don't forget to keep a bucket of water nearby for discarding used fireworks.

- Keep pets indoors: Pets tend to be quite frightened by fireworks—especially the loud, popping ones. In fact, some animals (like our miniature dachshund Miller) have to take sedatives every July Fourth. Just be aware of their fear, and show them a little extra love on that night.

MICHELLE MEDLOCK ADAMS is an award-winning writer and popular writers' conference speaker. Author of fifteen books, Michelle's latest releases include *No Boys Allowed! Devotions for Girls* (Zonderkidz, 2004), *Sparrow's New Song* (Ideals Children's Books, 2004), and *Daily Wisdom for Working Women* (Barbour Publishing, 2004). Michelle married her high school sweetheart, Jeff, and they have two daughters. Visit her at www.michellemedlockadams.com.

Harvest Home Celebration

CHERI LYNN COWELL

HAVE YOU READ articles about entertaining family and friends at Thanksgiving, Christmas, and New Year's and wonder how in the world people find the time? I know I have.

I wished there were a way to capture that holiday spirit at a less hectic time on the calendar so I could focus more on the people in my life. It seemed the more I struggled to focus on relationships rather than rushing around, the more I longed and prayed to find a way to take the pressure off.

The steam discharged from my holiday pressure cooker when I discovered the Jewish festivals or feasts. As I studied these Old Testament celebrations, I began to hear God telling me that my heart's desire could be found in bringing these ancient traditions to my friends and family—at another time of the year. This discovery has allowed me to spend relaxed and cherished time with those I love.

Of the six festivals God commanded the Israelites to celebrate, the Feast of Tabernacles or Booths or, as it is also called, the Festival of Ingathering, captures the best of Thanksgiving, New Year's, and the Christian Christmas. Celebrated today at the end of September or beginning of October, a Harvest Home Celebration becomes the perfect time to slow down and turn our attention to our family, friends, and faith.

Whether you choose to invite your family, a group of girlfriends, your Bible study group, or neighbors you wish to know better, this celebration can be as simple or elaborate as you wish to make it. Here I share suggestions for invitations, ways to decorate, and menu plans. Each Harvest Home Celebration will be different, but the core traditions borrowed from the Jewish Feast will be the same.

For your Harvest Home Celebration, you may wish to invite guests to bring their Bibles. If you possess a collection of family Bibles or a cherished Bible from your childhood, display these on your coffee table. As people gather, invite them to share stories of when they received their first Bibles or the significance of the Bible they brought with them. As they sit down for dinner, invite them to bring their Bibles with them. You may wish to give your guests the relevant Scriptures ahead of time so they will feel comfortable when reading them at the table.

As you will see in the Scriptures, elements from two of the ceremonies in the Jewish worship of the Feast can be used in your own home celebrations. The first, the nightly illumination of the Temple's Court of Women with gigantic candelabra that provided light for the nightly festivities, can be simply celebrated by reading the Scriptures as you light the candles in your dining area after you say grace.

The two names given to the Feast of Tabernacles reflect its dual meaning to the Israelites and its multiple layers of significance for us today. Leviticus details God's instructions for this feast with an explanation of the significance of the booths. For a complete description of the Feast of Tabernacles, see Leviticus 23:33–43.

SUGGESTED SCRIPTURES

Before grace is said: Deuteronomy 16:13–15 and Hebrews 13:15

At the lighting of the candles: Psalm 119:105 and John 8:12

As drink for the meal is poured: Isaiah 58:11 and John 7:37–41

When dessert is served: Proverbs 7:2 and Psalm 19:8–10

At the closing of the meal: Revelations 7:9–17 and John 14:2, 3

The second is the water-drawing ceremony, which was rich in symbolism and high drama. The water was drawn at the Pool of Siloam in a golden pitcher by a priest who carried it to the Temple accompanied by a procession of faithful worshipers. The water was poured over the altar while the people chanted to the accompaniment of flutes and the "great Hallel," consisting of Psalms 113 to 118. It was at the conclusion of this ceremony that Christ offered His living water (John 7:37).[1]

This symbolism can be achieved by serving in large golden pitchers one of the many fruit-flavored bottled waters available today. If you cannot find golden pitchers, tie large gold ribbons to the handle of your glass pitcher and to the stems of your guest's glasses.

The remaining verses listed in the Suggested Scriptures above allow us to glean the layers of symbolism and meaning God intended His people to receive from the Feast. The book of Exodus (23:16; 34:22) refers to the blessings harvest (calling the festival the Feast of the Ingathering).

Several ideas follow to stimulate your creative thinking for your Harvest Home Celebration. As you read each section, make note of the things you may already have that you can use to create this special event.

---

[1]Samuele Bacchiocchi, *God's Festivals in Scripture and History* (Berrien Springs, MI, Biblical Perspectives, 1996), from Web site www.biblicalperspectives.com.

Invitation Ideas

Invitations can be printed from your home computer or handmade with construction paper, scissors, and glue. Choose symbols of the fall harvest such as acorns, fall leaves, apples, or baskets of fruit to adorn the invitations. A visit to your local craft store will yield precut symbols, pictures, or embossed paper.

Be sure to answer the who, what, where, when, and why questions on the inside of the invite. The *why* question can be answered by including the Scripture verses from Deuteronomy 16. If you wish to invite guests to bring a dish to share for the meal, be sure to include that information as well as to ask them to bring their Bible.

Because this is something new for most people, you may wish to follow up with a phone call a few days later to answer questions. If your guests will be sharing in the reading of the Scriptures, this would be a good time to give them their parts.

Decorating Ideas

Whether you live in Florida as I do or in a state that has more of the natural fall touches, you can turn your home into a harvest home with a few simple touches. Begin at your front door by hanging a vine wreath decorated with colored leaves, fruits, and nuts. Use a leaf pattern to draw fall leaves on brown luncheon bags. Cut out the leaf designs and place a canning jar inside each bag with a candle to illuminate the walkway.

You may also wish to place a wheelbarrow in the front yard filled with hay and fall vegetables such as pumpkins, gourds, squash, potatoes, and corn. A yellow floodlight on the front door says "you are welcome" in a soft and gentle way.

As you enter the door, look for places to add a little fall color. Fill baskets with pinecones or tuck a metal bucket with apples among pine boughs.

Drape vines or branches of magnolias or fall-colored leaves over your fireplace mantle or along a sofa table. Add pinecones, nuts, and colorful fruit and vegetables to the display.

Large vegetable baskets picked up at the farmer's market can also be filled with hay and apples or fall flowers. Even an old vase filled with dried twigs can add to your harvest home display.

Finally, look for elements of water and candles to add to the dining area. Begin with the greenery, and then add the colorful fruits and vegetables. If you own a fountain, place it on a sideboard or corner table. If you don't have a fountain, cover the bottom of a tray or cookie sheet with black aquarium sand, place smooth stones randomly over the sand, and fill with water.

Cover the edges of the tray with greenery and place a candelabra or a stand of candlesticks around it. Use hollowed apples, oranges, and mini pumpkins for tea lights. Tie cinnamon sticks and raffia around the silverware-napkin bundles at each person's place setting. Print each guest's name on construction paper and tuck in a washed and dried pinecone placed on each person's plate as place cards.

Menu Ideas

Somehow, inviting guests to bring a dish to share makes this celebration feel more festive. I've found it best to tell my guests what meat we will be serving so they can plan a side dish to accompany it. Chicken or turkey is the traditional holiday food, but you may choose lamb, pork, or beef.

Included in the recipes is one of my favorite chicken dishes because it uses grapes, which look especially festive. For an appetizer, I serve my easy-to-make pumpkin soup in a hollowed pumpkin. To top off the evening, the baked stuffed apples are a Harvest Celebration all their own. Be sure to have most of your meal prepared ahead so you can spend time with your guests, which is the real purpose for this celebration.

CHERI'S EASY PUMPKIN SOUP

2	15 ounces cans pure pumpkin	$1/2$	teaspoon cinnamon
2	16 ounces cans chicken broth	1	teaspoon salt
2	tablespoons sugar	1	cup half and half
$1/2$	teaspoon nutmeg		

Bring all ingredients minus half and half to a boil, reduce heat to a simmer, and add half and half. Heat through and serve from a hollowed pumpkin.

HARVEST CHICKEN

1	large roaster (chicken)	3	tablespoons butter
1	cup cooked wild rice	1	cup honey mustard
$1/2$	cup minced onion	1	stick butter
2	cloves minced garlic		Clump of grapes
3	tablespoons thyme		

Sauté onion, garlic, and thyme in butter, add to wild rice and cool. Stuff chicken with rice mixture and tie legs together over the cavity. Place in roasting pan with remaining rice. Heat honey mustard and the stick of butter until butter is melted. Pour three-quarters of the mixture over the chicken. Bake at 350 degrees for $1\frac{1}{2}$ hours, basting every half hour with remaining mixture. The last 5 minutes add a clump of grapes to the roasting pan. When serving, place the grapes at the opening to the cavity as the rice pours forth.

BAKED STUFFED APPLES

1 small apple for every two guests (Gala, Fuji, and Nittany are good)	2 teaspoons cinnamon
	1 teaspoon cloves
	1 cup granola cereal
For every four apples:	3 tablespoons grated coconut
3 tablespoons butter	¼ cup orange blossom honey
2 tablespoons brown sugar	

Rinse apples, cut in half, and core. Place them in a baking dish. Melt butter in saucepan; add all ingredients except honey and coconut. Remove from heat, add honey and coconut. Fill apples with mixture. Cover with plastic wrap and microwave for 5 minutes. Place under broiler for 2 minutes, watching closely. Serve with whipped cream.

Children in the Harvest Home

If children will be included in your guest list, a few adjustments will need to be made. Be especially careful with candles and young children. You may also need to add some kid-friendly alternatives to the menu. Apple wedges make a good substitute for the soup, and the apple dessert will need to be cut up before serving. Children like to participate, so invite them to be your helpers by letting them don aprons and help serve.

Those who are older can light the candles and read Scripture. You may also add to your celebration by having participants join in a family craft project when they arrive. Make banners and add a processional to the beginning of the meal. Of course, the traditional bobbing for apples and pumpkin seed-spitting contests are always fun fall activities for older children.

As you and your guests join hands at the close of your meal and read from the book of Revelation, the fullness of God's love and grace will fill your hearts. You may wish to have verses 10 and 12 printed on cards so everyone

---

RESOURCES

God's Festivals in Scripture and History: Part 2: The Fall Festivals by Samuele Bacchiocchi, Biblical Perspectives, Berrien Springs, Michigan, 1996.

This is a superb resource with descriptions of the Old Testament practices and what they mean for us in light of New Testament teachings.

Celebrate the Feasts by Martha Zimmerman, Bethany House, Minneapolis, Minnesota, 1981.

This book provides wonderful, practical ideas to celebrate a family-friendly feast.

---

can join in saying those parts. If you can memorize verses 16 and 17, and are able to make eye contact with your guests as you say those marvelous words, "Never again will they hunger; never again will they thirst. The sun will not beat upon them, nor any scorching heat. For the Lamb at the center of the throne will be their shepherd; he will lead them to springs of living water. And God will wipe away every tear from their eyes," it will be a memory your guests will never forget. And when the dishes are piled in the sink, your friends and family have gone home for the evening, and you have kicked off your shoes and sunk into the sofa, I believe you will find this may have become your favorite holiday of the year.

CHERI LYNN COWELL balances the roles of wife, work, and a growing speaking and writing career which leaves Cheri little time for cooking and entertaining. "If it doesn't cook in *thirty* minutes, it's not for me," she often quips. Cheri's love for serving others is evident in her popular *Recipes For Life* presentation, a soon-to-be-published book. Visit her at www.gardensgateministries.com.

Thanksgiving

Jean Ann Duckworth

THANKSGIVING IS a wonderful occasion filled with family, food, and blessings. But it also can be an extremely exhausting and stressful occasion. Falling in the middle of the workweek, we feel overwhelmed trying to juggle our regular responsibilities with the added task of preparing a very labor-intensive meal. Unlike Christmas, where we have the opportunity to prepare for the big day weeks if not months in advance (although few of us take advantage of this), the food preparation of Thanksgiving does not allow us to work very far ahead. The items making up our menu must be fresh and hot. This means we often spend the week before the holiday shopping for the meal, only to spend the holiday itself in the kitchen preparing a meal that will be consumed in a fraction of the time it took to prepare. It's almost enough to cause you to hide in bed Thanksgiving Day.

The situation is not that grim, however. The majority of the stress caused by Thanksgiving is self-produced. By taking a new approach to the holiday, you will not only reduce your level of stress, but you also will increase the time you have to sit back and enjoy the holiday. There are just a few simple things you need to do to make your Thanksgiving more enjoyable.

> "... Give thanks to him and praise his name. For the LORD is good and his love endures forever ..." (Psalm 100:4, 5)

Plan

The last trick-or-treater has come and gone. You have thrown the jack-o-lantern in the trash and changed the calendar from October to November. Now is the time to sit down and develop a plan of action. Your theme for Thanksgiving needs to be "work smarter, not harder." Follow a systematic plan of action and you will be amazed how everything falls into place.

Guest List

Develop your guest list. Until you know how many people will be sitting at your Thanksgiving table, you cannot go another step. All too often, we jump right into the planning process before we have a firm grasp on the size of our event. Preparing a dinner for six is much different than preparing for a dinner for twenty-five. Make a list of everyone you know will be attending and then make a list of everyone you think *might* attend. Take the time to make a few phone calls. Your goal is not to get a solid commitment for dinner reservations, but to simply get a rough head count.

Menu

Once you have a rough idea how many guests will be coming for dinner, decide on a menu. Some families like variety of dishes while others want a large quantity of a few dishes. When we were first married, my husband and I would invite coworkers to share Thanksgiving dinner with us. The first year, I put out a huge spread, offering a variety of vegetables and side dishes.

I ended up with *lots* of leftovers. Our guests were mostly men—young men. They wanted lots of meat, plenty of potatoes, a spoonful of green beans, rolls, and pie. I learned quickly to make a larger quantity of fewer dishes. Your guests may be the exact opposite. Some people like to choose from a variety of dishes, taking a sample of everything. Do your guests go for variety or quantity? While a few leftovers are nice, you don't want to fill your refrigerator with items that no one is ever going to eat. When in doubt, go for quantity rather than selection.

If time is a factor for you, then stick to a few basic dishes and make plenty of each. It takes less energy to make large quantities of five dishes than to make small quantities of ten dishes. Remember to work smarter, not harder.

Quantity

After creating your menu, you need to determine how much food it will take to feed everyone. Here are some guidelines:

TURKEY: You can follow the tried-and-true formula: 1½–2 pounds of turkey per guest. Or you can follow my formula. I believe the turkey is the centerpiece of the meal. Therefore, I begin with a 20+-plus pound turkey. Once my guest list goes to eight or more, I add another large turkey. I know extra turkey will *never* go to waste in my house. Turkey is so inexpensive during the holidays that it makes sense to purchase a large bird. Leftovers can be frozen if necessary.

MASHED POTATOES: You should plan on two medium-size potatoes per person. If you're not serving a variety of dishes, you might need to add two to three potatoes to the final count.

VEGETABLES: Begin with two vegetables for the first six guests and add one vegetable for every four additional guests.

DESSERTS: Desserts should be determined in groups of four; for every four guests, add a dessert. You might want to begin with two different kinds of pies to offer a selection. Whether you expand on your variety or choose to increase the quantity of the original pies is up to you.

Shopping List

You have created your guest list, decided on your menu, and determined the quantities of each dish you plan to serve. Now is the time to develop your shopping list. But it's only the beginning of November? True, you do not need to shop for a few weeks. However, by making your list early and referring to it often, you avoid forgetting items (like butter) and you also give yourself the opportunity to take advantage of sales that will come up in the weeks before Thanksgiving.

To-do List

Next, create your to-do list. Take your time to develop a detailed list of everything that needs to be done before, during, and after the big meal. Remember that no task is too small or too obvious. Of course the table needs to be set, but put it down anyway. Take an inventory of the items you need. Is your good tablecloth worse for wear? Is it clean? Does the silver need to be polished? Do you have enough dinner plates for eighteen? Is your table large enough to seat everyone? Give yourself time to think these things out.

Delegation

Once you have a list of everything that needs to be done, determine which items you want to handle yourself. Some of you may be confused by this thought. You may be under the mistaken impression that you must do everything yourself for the day to be a success. Or, you might believe people will think less of you if you ask them for help. Well, the day will be great regardless of who sets the table and people will think what they think, so stop worrying about it. Your goal is to have enough energy to enjoy Thanksgiving. Determine the tasks you *want* to do yourself and delegate the rest. Thanksgiving is a family affair and nothing says family like everyone contributing to the day.

When making a list of all that needs to be done, don't stop with the serving of the meal. There's no reason you should spend the rest of the afternoon/evening in the kitchen up to your elbows in dishwater. Include on your list all the tasks that need to be done after the meal, and determine who will do these tasks. If everyone does their part, cleanup will take no time at all.

Spend time sitting at the table with a pad of paper. Put the majority of your time and energy in the planning process, and the rest of the preparations will flow smoothly.

Purchase

You have created your initial shopping list. Go over it thoroughly. Compare your list to your menu. Make sure you have included the ingredients you need to complete your menu. Thanksgiving requires a lot of butter. You might remember to buy enough for the dinner table and forget how much you need to baste the turkey and mash the potatoes. Do an inventory of your refrigerator, freezer, and cupboard. Check the spice cabinet. For example, if you only use sage at Thanksgiving, you may want a new jar.

Once your shopping list is complete, always carry it with you. When the store ads come out each week, check to see what is on sale. On your list, write the sale price of items you need. This makes an easy reference when you shop. Avoid combining your holiday list with your everyday list. If you buy an item for everyday use and then cross it off your holiday list as well, you might not have enough when Thanksgiving arrives.

Follow your list. Check off items as you buy. Some things can be purchased two to three weeks in advance. Others need to be purchased no more than a week in advance. Find a way to distinguish your Thanksgiving purchases from the rest of your groceries. Make sure everyone in the family knows your marking system.

Choose a day in the week before Thanksgiving to do your major shopping. Take help with you. You may need more than one cart and it is nice to have assistance with the lifting and loading. Try to shop at a time when the shelves are full and the store is empty.

Take time to organize your shopping list, inventory your refrigerator and shelves, and study the ads. You will save not only money and time, but also your sanity.

Prepare

You have made your lists and done your shopping. Now it is time to prepare for the big event. Before you peel a potato or stuff a turkey, sit down first and create a timetable. Knowing how long it takes to prepare dishes saves you frustration when you only have one oven and four items that need to bake. Coordinate your cooking schedule so everything gets on the table at the same time, hot and ready to eat. Here are a few tips to help you set up your schedule:

- If you're preparing two turkeys, cook one the night before Thanksgiving. Roast that one without the stuffing. Allow it to cool, then slice it, wrap it, and store it. You might want to place the slices on a platter, ready to serve. Heat in the microwave before serving.
- Time your turkey to finish roasting ninety minutes before dinner. Turkey needs to cool before it is sliced. The stuffing will keep it warm.
- Using cooking bags requires less roasting time for the turkey. It also means you do not have to baste the bird. Be sure to open the bag right after removing the turkey from the oven so it does not stick to the bird.
- Begin peeling potatoes just after you take the turkey out of the oven. They do not need long to cook. Potatoes should be cooked until just tender. Cooking them too long makes them pasty.

- Use a Crock-Pot to cook vegetables such as green beans. They can be put on to simmer on low and left to cook throughout the day.
- While you want to bake pies in advance, you might want an extra pumpkin pie to bake at the last minute. The aroma will fill your house.
- Save yourself the aggravation. Use premade gravy. It can be heated in the microwave just before serving.
- Mashing the potatoes should be one of the last things you do. As you mash the potatoes, have someone else begin putting the vegetables and gravy on the table.
- Put the rolls in the oven right before you mash the potatoes. Remember to set the timer.

Presentation

What a wonderful feeling for a hostess to have her guests walk into the room and marvel over her beautiful table. It looks as if it took hours to prepare. It does not have to take any time at all. You just need to work smarter to create a beautiful presentation.

Set the table the night before. Put out place settings, serving pieces, and salt and pepper. Cover with a sheet to keep clean and neat.

- Put a slip of paper in/on each serving piece so you remember what goes on each. This will help guests who offer to help.
- Use a pie for your centerpiece. Place a wreath of autumn leaves in the center of the table. Place a cake stand in the center of the wreath. Place a pie or other dessert on the cake stand for a delicious centerpiece.
- If you have prepared two turkeys, remove the stuffing from the second turkey and place the unsliced turkey on the table.
- You may use disposable tableware if you wish. Yes, paper plates. This will save you time on cleanup. Choose an autumn design that accents your table.

- If you're hosting a large group, consider serving buffet style. Set up a beverage table off to the side. Fellowship is the most important ingredient when entertaining. Creating an informal but elegant occasion allows your guests to visit, relax, and enjoy themselves.

Party

This means you. It is time for you to party. You're the most important guest at your event. If you do not enjoy yourself, then no one will enjoy themselves. People come to your house to enjoy themselves. Your attitude will ensure that they do. Take a short nap while the turkey is roasting. Leave time for a nice relaxing bath. Take your time getting ready. Invite one or two guests to come early to help you with a few last-minute things or just keep you company while you finish up. When the doorbell rings, take a deep

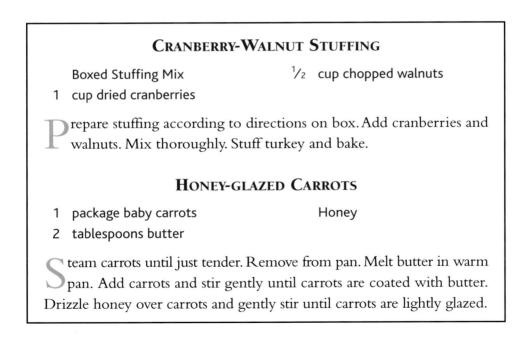

CRANBERRY-WALNUT STUFFING

Boxed Stuffing Mix $\frac{1}{2}$ cup chopped walnuts
1   cup dried cranberries

Prepare stuffing according to directions on box. Add cranberries and walnuts. Mix thoroughly. Stuff turkey and bake.

HONEY-GLAZED CARROTS

1   package baby carrots   Honey
2   tablespoons butter

Steam carrots until just tender. Remove from pan. Melt butter in warm pan. Add carrots and stir gently until carrots are coated with butter. Drizzle honey over carrots and gently stir until carrots are lightly glazed.

breath and smile. It's Thanksgiving and you have so many things to be thankful for.

JEAN ANN DUCKWORTH and her husband, Terry, are the owners of The Extreme Diva that provides information and products to simplify home entertaining. The Extreme Diva is always entertaining at www.theextremediva.com. Jean Ann and Terry live in Southern California.

Christmas

EVA MARIE EVERSON

IF YOU'RE anything like me, God has blessed you with a heart full of friends. A blessing indeed, but come Christmas—with merchants telling you to "Buy! Buy! Buy!" and your own heart's desire being to gift each friend in a special way—you may find your purse strings pulling a bit too tightly.

Christmas giving to friends does not have to mean a trip to the poorhouse. Several years ago, financially strapped yet overflowing with friends, my husband and I decided to give the gift of a special evening. To usher in the "most wonderful time of the year," we hosted a party early in the season. We invited our closest friends, asking each one to bring a beverage and a contribution of a cheese tray, fruit tray, dessert, or fun food. We would provide the atmosphere, wassail, coffee, meat trays, nuts, and after-dinner mints. The result has been the most talked-about and anticipated party of all those we hold dear. The good news is that this is not an idea difficult to bring to fruition. Anyone can do it, no matter how financially or time strapped they may be.

One Month Before

Get your invitations ready. If finances are really tight, you have the choice of making your invitation personal by picking up the phone. Or, if the majority of your friends are Internet-bound, you can send a creative and festive invitation via cyberspace.

The invitations should include the following:

Date

Strive to mark your calendar for the first Saturday of December; otherwise, you'll find your guests trying to balance themselves between your party and a company party or any number of other social engagements the season affords. Saturday is typically better than Friday because of work. You want your guests to be well rested rather than dragging from the day.

Time

Because you'll be serving plenty of food, 7 P.M. is a perfect time for the guests to arrive. It's not too early; it's not too late. Because of the time of year, it will already be dark outside, which means your house and the houses near you should be bright with holiday lights and decorations. As for the party's end, we've always left it open. Our guests typically begin leaving around 10 P.M., with a few remaining until 11. This group usually lingers for hours, chatting and laughing. What fun!

Place

Your home, of course, but don't expect that to always be obvious. You'll want your guests to know this gift is coming from your home to their hearts.

Dress

Encourage your guests to be festive. This is an opportunity to dress up, though tuxes are not expected from the men nor are gowns for the ladies. Dressing up becomes the "fun" of the evening. You can even have a little contest for best-dressed couple.

Contribution

Let the invitations show you'll be providing coffee, wassail, and meat dishes. Suggest that guests bring the drink of their choice and a fruit, cheese, or dessert tray.

Etc., etc., etc.

You might want to sponsor a "canned good" gift for the "entrance fee." The invitations should show that the canned goods will be taken to a food pantry, homeless shelter, or women's shelter.

RSVP

Be sure to have your guests RSVP, letting you know what they will be bringing. This is a great way to avoid unpleasant surprises on the evening of your party.

One to Two Weeks Before

Begin doing what you would be doing anyway—decorating your home with a Christmas tree or trees, garland, nativity scenes, and so on. Over the years, I have gathered more holiday decorations than I can ever begin to display, but if you're limited, keep the focus on the tree.

In our home, every room displays the season. Beds are topped with seasonal throws, and holiday pillows grace the beds, the sofa, and chairs. Christmas towels are in the baths and kitchen. Snowman table sets (purchased for next to nothing at deep discount stores) decorate the kitchen table. A nativity set adorns the mantel over the fireplace. There are candles (again, you can find these at inexpensive prices) and baskets of pinecones sprayed gold and scented with cinnamon. Other baskets spill over with holiday greeting cards from loved ones. The front door has a festive wreath, and each inside door displays large red velvet bows. Another idea for inside doors is to have a large holiday ribbon running vertically along its center and then, using two-sided tape, attach your greeting cards.

You should have heard from your guests by one week before your party. Check your menu and then make a list of the things you'll need to purchase.

✿ One Day Before

If you have enough silver, crystal, and china for your guests, now is the time to get them out, polish them, wash them, dry them, and display them. We have both a kitchen table and a dining room table, so the dining room table is where we place these necessities. I've been known to take ordinary water glasses, tie a ribbon around each, and use them as holders for my spoons, knives and forks. Plates are placed on one part of the table, crystal on another, and don't forget the napkins. If you don't have enough linen napkins for the number of guests you've invited, purchase paper dinner napkins. I prefer the white "formal" napkins, but you may want to have those with a holiday print.

If you do not have enough silver, crystal, or china, then head to a store that sells things for a dollar or less and purchase plastic and paper products in fun seasonal colors. It won't be as formal but, believe me, your guests won't care. Dim the lights, light the candles, and they'll never say a word. This party is not about impressing people. It's about the joyous gift of friendship.

Make sure your furniture is dusted and your floors are clean, and pay attention to the baths. You'll want to make certain there are hand towels in the guest bath. (You can always purchase paper guest hand towels if you don't have enough of the real thing.) Your wastebasket should be empty and close by. As a final touch in the guest bath, have bath-size throwaway cups and a decanter of mouthwash. I was fortunate to find a whiskey decanter at a yard sale, which I brought home, scalded in the dishwasher, and then filled with mouthwash. A small placard stating *For Our Guests* can be placed in front of it. With all the eating and the close talking, your friends will thank you for this thoughtful addition.

Finally, get out your holiday CDs or tapes, and bring a portable player into the center of the place your guests will be gathering. We have satellite TV, which affords us a "holiday music" channel. Make sure the music isn't too loud for the party, however. You'll want to give atmosphere, not a concert.

🎵 The Day of the Party

It won't be easy, but try to rest a bit before you have to get ready. Your friends are only hours from arriving and, if you're like me, you'll be too excited to sleep. But try.

You'll want to prepare your food at a time based on what you're providing. Because your dining table is filled with plates and so forth, you'll need a place for the food and drinks. Here are some suggestions:

- Clean away your kitchen countertops and utilize the space.
- It you have a kitchen table, use this for either the food or drinks.
- If you have room for a third table somewhere in your home, try that. Because I live in Florida and the weather is always warm, we open up our screened patio, line it with white lights, and have a long table out there for the drinks.

A few hours before your guests arrive, take a hot shower or relaxing bath and then dress and primp. A half hour before, walk through the house and check on things. Is everything as you want it to be? Don't stress . . . this is just a walk-through. Are the tree lights on? Music playing? Wassail simmering atop the stove, emitting the most welcoming of fragrances? Coffee beginning to brew? Sugar and creamer out? If you live in a cold climate, is a fire crackling in the fireplace? Do you have holiday potpourri in bowls throughout the house, making every room welcoming?

Five to ten minutes before your guests arrive, dim the lights and light the candles. Take a deep breath, exhale, and . . . *is that a car door shutting?*

❧ During and after the Party

Enjoy yourself. Meet guests at the door and, if you're so inclined, have a camera close by and take photos. You'll be glad you did in years to come.

Don't forget to mix and mingle. Introduce those of your friends who don't know one another. At one point in the evening, if one of your guests (or yourself!) is musically inclined, sing a few carols.

Remember, no cleaning up while your guests are still in your home. Jesus said, "Tomorrow will take care of itself." Tomorrow surely shall . . . and that's the day for cleaning. You'll be tired, so don't push yourself. It's important that this is fun for you, too. Last night's party will be talked about for a long time as an enjoyable event, a gift from your home to the hearts of your friends.

❧ Christmas Parties and Gatherings[1]

A Christmas gift from the heart begins with your invitation. Its very being says, "I like you, I appreciate you, I want your company at this party!" Don't you feel wonderful when you get an invitation? I do. A party can be:

A Large Gathering with Appetizers, Cookies, and Desserts

Use name tags for a party this size. Save time for singing Christmas carols. It's old-fashioned and filled with Christmas love!

A Neighborhood Progressive Dinner

Four stops for this party: hors d'oeuvres, salad, main course, and dessert.

Parties for People Who Might Not Have One

The need for love, care, and celebration is with us always, but especially at Christmas. And especially for those who are isolated from Christmas activity. Your church can help. Be sure to include a tangible gift such as backpacks for children; food boxes for the hungry; or pen, paper, and stamps for the elderly. Follow the light of Jesus in your loving service.

Happy Birthday Baby Jesus Parties for Children

A tea party for girls and a pizza party for boys. Have a cake for the new-born King and sing, sing, sing "Happy Birthday to You!"

Work Parties—No "Bah, Humbug" Here!

Maybe you're not the party planner, but you'd still like to do something "sweet" for Christmas. How about bringing Christmas candy to work beginning December 1? My daughter Candy loves to celebrate . . . everything. A basket of wrapped (no germs this way) candy sits on her desk at work for every holiday. Let's just say she's never lonely!

A Christmas Luncheon

A dear friend has an annual Christmas luncheon with good food, a small gift, and her unabashed love. There's always a Christmas discussion question to draw us into conversation and mutual blessing. For example: What gift did the Lord give to you this year? Or, what gift have you given Him? We run the gamut of emotions, the most prevalent being joy!

Prepare the food if you have the time. If not, and your budget allows, make "creative purchases." Begin with good bread or rolls. Then buy several chicken Caesar salads (one per person is always too much), toss them together in a large salad bowl, and viola . . . Christmas luncheon is served. A "Yule Log" ice cream cake makes a great dessert. For an extra special touch, put whipped cream in a small bowl and serve it with the coffee and sugar.

Have gentle music playing, the fire going (only if you have a fireplace!), hot apple cider, and a little something to munch. The table discussion could revolve around "the reason for the season" or my favorite, "What's your best childhood Christmas memory?"

You may wish to ask each lady to bring one wrapped gift within a certain price range for a gift exchange. This is really fun, and it's nice to leave with a little memento from the time spent together.—Dolley Carlson, *Christmas Gifts from the Heart*

EVA MARIE EVERSON is a nationally recognized speaker and the author of a number of books, including *The Shadows Trilogy* (Barbour). She is a feature writer at www.Crosswalk.com and a contributor to *The Godly Business Woman* magazine. She and her husband live in Florida. Eva Marie can be contacted at www.evamarieeverson.com.

30

CHAPTER

New Year's Day

JANE JARRELL

NEW YEAR is like a fresh canvas—clean, unmarked, and full of potential. Party planning can be just as full of possibilities—if that plan is foolproof. The thought of a party squeezed into an already packed schedule can lead one to throw in the reservations and forget the gathering.

As playwright and humorist Jean Kerr wrote, "Having a party is something like having a baby. The fact that you got through the last one alive is not somehow reassuring now." In the 1957 edition of *Etiquette,* Emily Post describes the endless trials of the perfect hostess: "If a cook leaves (my cook never showed up), the hostess will have to organize a last-minute picnic. Unless she 'is actually unable to stand up,' a hostess must keep any physical ailments hush-hush."

Honestly, there must be a happy medium between these two points. When the New Year beckons, keep in mind the KISS method—Keep It Simple Sister. If the host and hostess cannot sit down and enjoy the meal along with their guests, then the "simple" has been squeezed out of the experience. I once saw a cartoon that depicted an extremely harried lady making her grocery list, rushing through the store, unloading her wares, chopping, stirring, baking, and, finally, sitting at the head of her long table surrounded

> Share your life, and find the finest joy man can know. Do not be stingy with your heart. Get out of your self into the lives of others, and new life will flow into you—share and share alike. —JOSEPH FORT NEWTON

by guests with her weary head flat in the middle of her plate. No one wants a martyr as a hostess.

The Setting

Try entering your home as a guest, going out the front door and taking a look at what your guests will see.

Smell

This is usually the first thing a guest notices. Make it good. If you won't have pleasant dinner aromas when your guests arrive, place a head of garlic in the oven to slow roast.

Sound

Good, relaxing music sets the atmosphere. Find some tunes that match your occasion.

Sight

Vary the setting. Have appetizers in the foyer, or on the front porch, or on the coffee table in the den. Fresh flowers always say this is a special time together.

Taste

Buy great groceries. Fresh is best. Use simple yet delicious recipes.

✍ **The Games and Activities**

Guess the Cartoon Caption

Assemble an assortment of favorite cartoons. Cut the captions from the cartoons and keep them in a separate envelope. (You may want to photocopy the cartoons first just in case you think you won't remember the captions.) When the guests arrive, each person receives a caption or a cartoon and a pin with which to affix the paper to his or her clothing. Guests must then circulate and find their "match."

Life Verse for the New Year

Each New Year offers a great time for spiritual renewal. Ask guests to think about what verse they would most like to live out in the upcoming year and why. Offer small sheets of paper or index cards for the guests to write down their verses. For instance, "But seek first his kingdom and his righteousness, and all these things will be given to you as well" (Matt. 6:33). Why will I try to live this verse daily? If I am seeking God, I have a better chance of living in obedience, which offers peace in the midst of life's pressures.

The Table

Simple things offer pleasure. Look for twigs with an interesting shape, cut out paper snowflakes with your children, pick and scatter flower petals. One of my favorite rules for creating a memorable occasion is to use materials that are readily available—nothing too contrived. In autumn, I use a large terra cotta pot full of white and orange baby pumpkins. In winter, I use as a centerpiece lots and lots of candles, unscented so as not to interfere with the food smells. In the spring, I use seven skinny clear glass vases, from the dollar store, and place a Gerber daisy in each vase. During the summer, I use teapots filled with fresh lavender and white geraniums. Always remember, mixing and matching works.

A meal on New Year's Day often calls for casual, make-ahead, easy-to-tote-to-the-television foods because college football is often the lead attraction, at least for some of your guests. Find or borrow baskets of different sizes and shapes. Use throw-away platters or plates that can be easily placed into the baskets, and set up a basket buffet. Use rattan paper plate holders. Flatware placed in a napkin can be tied with raffia several days prior to the party and then placed in a basket and set next to the plates at the starting point of the buffet.

The Buffet

When offering a buffet, you're off the hook on plate presentation. You can concentrate on making the buffet attractive. Try intermingling trays full of different sized white candles among your baskets and throughout your entertaining area. If your paperwhites or poinsettias are still standing after Christmas, they work perfectly for added color.

The Menu

Here is a complete make-ahead menu; however, if the thought of cooking all this food kicks the relaxation right out of your short break, try using a similar menu with the quick-fix option.

Pecan-crusted Chicken with Blackberry Ketchup
Corn and Black-eyed Pea Confetti
Three Potato Salad with Bacon
Five-layer Salad
Easy Bundt Bread
Spicy Brown Sugar Angel Food Cake with Cinnamon Cream
Flourless Chocolate Torte
Cinnamon Snowflakes
Flavored Waters with Fresh Orange Slices

PECAN-CRUSTED CHICKEN

Serves 8 to 10

3 pounds chicken breast fillets	$\frac{1}{4}$ cup cream cheese
$\frac{1}{4}$ teaspoon salt	1 teaspoon mustard
$\frac{1}{4}$ teaspoon pepper	1 teaspoon fresh thyme
3 teaspoons butter	1 cup pecans, chopped
$\frac{1}{4}$ cup mushrooms, chopped	$\frac{1}{2}$ cup breadcrumbs
$\frac{1}{4}$ cup green onion, chopped	3 tablespoons butter, melted
	pinch of parsley

1. On a hard surface, pound chicken, sprinkle with salt and pepper; set aside.
2. In a small skillet, melt butter. Add mushrooms and onion, sauté until tender. Cool.
3. Mix cream cheese, mustard, and thyme. Spread on the pieces of chicken and fold each fillet over, pressing the edges to seal.
4. Mix pecans, breadcrumbs, and parsley.
5. Dip chicken into remaining butter; roll each piece in pecan mixture to coat evenly.
6. Bake in a greased baking dish at 375 degrees for 35 minutes.

BLACKBERRY KETCHUP

Makes 1 cup

$\frac{3}{4}$ cup frozen blackberries	$\frac{1}{4}$ teaspoon ground cloves
3 tablespoons apple vinegar	$\frac{1}{4}$ teaspoon ground ginger
$\frac{1}{2}$ cup water	$\frac{1}{8}$ teaspoon cayenne pepper
3 tablespoons dark brown sugar	$\frac{1}{4}$ teaspoon salt
	2 teaspoons unsalted butter

1. Mix berries, vinegar, and water in a saucepan, and bring the mixture to a boil. Lower and simmer for 10 minutes. Sieve out the seeds, rub out berry pulp, and return the mixture to saucepan.
2. Mix remaining ingredients, and simmer 30 minutes until thicker. Pour into jar and seal. Refrigerate.

FIVE-LAYER SALAD

Serves 8 to 10

1 head iceberg or favorite lettuce
1 bunch carrots, grated
1 (10-ounce) package tiny peas, thawed

Dressing:

1½ cups mayonnaise
1 cup sour cream
Salt to taste
Pepper to taste

2 cups cheddar cheese, grated
1 pound bacon, crisply fried and crumbled
1 bunch green onions, tops only, chopped

Optional ingredients:

Bell pepper, celery, tomato, water chestnuts, sliced almonds, fresh mushrooms, and hard-boiled eggs, baked and shredded chicken, fresh spinach, red leaf lettuce, and avocado.

Wash, drain, and tear lettuce into pieces. In a large bowl, layer one half of the lettuce. Then layer carrots, peas, more lettuce, dressing, cheese, green onion, and bacon. Repeat layers if using a large bowl.

Prepare one day in advance. Wrap and refrigerate. Salad may either be tossed before serving or served as is. This stays fresh for several days because the dressing seals the lettuce mixture.

CORN AND BLACK-EYED PEA CONFETTI

Serves 6

1 (17-ounce) can whole kernel corn
1 (17-ounce) can black-eyed peas
¼ teaspoon ground ginger
¼ teaspoon dried mustard
¼ cup sugar

¼ cup vinegar
2 tablespoons minced green onion
2 tablespoons red pepper, chopped
1 tablespoon cilantro, chopped

1. Combine ginger, mustard, sugar, vinegar, and water in medium bowl; stir until thoroughly blended.
2. Add corn, black-eyed peas, onions, red pepper, and cilantro, stirring to combine.
3. Cover and refrigerate until chilled.

THREE POTATO SALAD WITH BACON

Serves 6 to 8

3	golden potatoes
6	new potatoes
1	medium sweet potato
$\frac{1}{2}$	cup celery, thinly sliced
1	large red-skinned apple, cored and diced

$\frac{1}{2}$	cup mayonnaise
1	teaspoon mustard
$\frac{1}{2}$	teaspoon orange peel, grated
2	tablespoons crisply cooked bacon, crumbled

1. Place potatoes in a 3 to 4 quart pan. Cover with water and bring to a boil over high heat. Cover, reduce heat, and cook until tender— about 20 minutes. Check potatoes often, because some will cook faster than others and may need to be removed. Drain.
2. When potatoes are cool, peel and cut them into $\frac{1}{2}$" cubes.
3. In a bowl, combine potatoes, celery, and apple.
4. In a small bowl, stir together mayonnaise, mustard, orange peel, and bacon.
5. Pour mayo mixture over potatoes; stir to combine.
6. Cover and refrigerate overnight.

EASY BUNDT BREAD

Makes 12 thick slices

3	cans of Pillsbury crescent rolls

1	stick margarine, melted

1. Preheat oven to 350 degrees.
2. Open each can of rolls, but do not unroll the dough.
3. Lay each roll of dough in the bundt pan, ends touching. Pinch ends together, making a complete ring of dough.
4. Pour melted margarine over dough.
5. Bake at 350 for 30–45 minutes until bread is golden brown.
6. Remove from oven; let cool in pan a few minutes before slicing.

SPICY BROWN SUGAR ANGEL FOOD CAKE
WITH CINNAMON CREAM

Serves 12

13 egg whites	1 cup cake flour, sifted
1½ teaspoons cream of tartar	1½ cups brown sugar
¼ teaspoon salt	1½ teaspoons vanilla
	2 teaspoons pumpkin pie spice

1. Place egg whites in a mixing bowl and begin beating, gradually adding cream of tartar and salt. Beat until soft peaks form.
2. Add brown sugar and vanilla. Beat well.
3. Sprinkle flour over egg white mixture ¼ cup at a time, beating well after each addition.
4. Add pumpkin pie spice.
5. Pour batter into a 10-inch tube pan and bake at 375 degrees for 30 to 35 minutes, or until cake springs back from your touch.
6. Invert pan and cool for 40 minutes. Loosen cake from sides of pan using a narrow metal spatula.
7. Drizzle cake with cinnamon cream.

CINNAMON CREAM

2 cups whipping cream, whipped	1½ teaspoons cinnamon
2 tablespoons powdered sugar	

Mix cream and sugar together. Slather on cake. Sprinkle with cinnamon.

FLOURLESS CHOCOLATE TORTE

7 ounces semi-sweet chocolate	1 cup sugar
½ cup coffee	4 eggs, beaten
8 ounces unsalted butter	

1. Melt chocolate and coffee together over low heat.
2. Stir in sugar.

3. Cut butter into 6-8 pieces. Gradually stir into chocolate mixture.

4. Remove pan from heat. Beat in eggs just until blended.

5. Spray an 8-inch springform pan with cooking spray. Pour mixture into the pan and bake for 35 to 40 minutes, or just until set. The center of the cake may still be a little runny.

6. Chill. Cake is easiest to cut when cold, but should be served at room temperature.

CINNAMON SNOWFLAKES

Soft flour tortillas
$\frac{1}{2}$ stick butter, melted

$\frac{1}{2}$ cup sugar
1 teaspoon cinnamon

1. Fold the flour tortillas into fourths; using kitchen scissors cut triangle shapes into the tortillas. (This is just like making the paper snowflakes in grade school.)

2. Combine sugar and cinnamon.

3. Brush tortilla with melted butter and sprinkle with sugar mixture.

4. Bake at 350 degrees for 8 minutes or until golden brown.

Quick-fix Menu

Harried and hurried, but still want to share a big hooray for the New Year? Try this simple quick-fix option. Ask each guest to bring his or her favorite dip. Suddenly, appetizers fill your home and you did not shop for the ingredients!

- Fried chicken strips (purchased from the grocery store), assorted dipping sauces
- Store-bought black-eyed pea dip, plus other favorites
- Assortment of chips
- Bag salads; add freshly grated carrots, zucchini, and tomatoes. Top with grated cheese and honey roasted peanuts.
- Store-purchased sourdough bread loaves

Ice Cream Sundae Bar

Pre-scoop a variety of ice cream flavors, place on a cookie sheet and then back into the freezer to refreeze. Once frozen in the scoop shape, place in a large bowl. When it is dessert time set out bowls of toppings and the large bowl of ice cream scoops.

JANE JARRELL is the author of twelve books and the coauthor of twenty others. She began her career with *Southern Living* magazine as a coordinator and emcee for cooking shows throughout the South. Jane worked for Neiman Marcus as the menu, recipe, and advertising coordinator for thirty-five restaurants. She is a food stylist, writer, speaker, wife, and mother. Her current book is *Secrets of a Midlife Mom* (NavPress). In 2005, W Publishing will release *The Frazzled Factor, Relief for Working Moms*. Visit www.janejarrell.net.

Recipe Index

THANK YOU!

We want to personally thank the readers of *The Godly Business Woman Magazine* for your continuous support. The feedback that we have received over the past five years inspired the creation and ultimate publication of *The Godly Business Woman Magazine Guide to Cooking and Entertainment.* Just like our magazine, *The Godly Business Woman Magazine Guide to Cooking and Entertainment* was written to educate, inspire, and motivate Godly businesswomen in effectively reaching out to others.

As our readers have shared time and again, *The Godly Business Woman Magazine* is the magazine for today's "busy" woman! Balancing family, and, spirituality are some of the top concerns of Christian women. These and other topics are addressed in each issue.

The goal of *The Godly Business Woman Magazine* is to encourage women to be all they can be through Jesus Christ. Our mission is to be a resource on which women can depend, and to shed light on God's view of the responsibilities we've been given. We feel very blessed and are so thankful that God is using both the magazine and this book to meet the needs of women everywhere.

If you would like additional information, or if you would like to subscribe to the magazine, please call 1-800-560-1090 or visit the Web site at www.godlybusinesswoman.com.

Jackson Family – Bottom, from left to right: Trent Varnadoe, Alexsia Varnadoe, Royce Jackson, Kathleen Jackson, Rusty and Michelle Varnadoe.

Davison Family – Bottom, from left to right: Ellie, Tracey Top, from left to right: Caleb and Andy Davison